GRACE
BEYOND BARS

SENTENCED TO 100 YEARS, FREED BY FAITH:
A TESTAMENT OF GOD'S POWER

RANDALL WHITE

FROM INMATE TO MENTOR, INSPIRING
OTHERS TO BREAK FREE

BUILD OUR KINGDOM PUBLISHING
—— BUILD OUR KINGDOM.COM ——

Grace Beyond Bars

1st Edition January 2025 First Printing
ISBN for paperback: 978-1-964203-15-7
Build Our Kingdom Publishing, LLC. 560 Main St, Stroudsburg, PA 18360
Edited by: Randall White & Allen Brown

Table of Contents

Every Book You Purchase Helps Build the Kingdom!

Every book you purchase on BuildOurKingdom.com donates up to 30% to the church of your choice. Simply visit BuildOurKingdom.com, explore our growing library of books, and support the Kingdom with every purchase.

Dedication

To Mom and Dad, Thank You for Your unwavering support and belief in my dreams and ability. Thank You for always encouraging me to think big. Your guidance and love has carried me through life. This book would not be possible without the wisdom You Guys imparted in me. Mom I still remember coming home from my first day of school and You sitting down with me and helping me to read through the whole first grade primer.

Love and miss You guys.

~ Randy ~

Acknowledgments

I first of all want to thank the Lord Jesus Christ for showing me His love for me and power towards me at the times of my darkest moments.

I want to thank my nephew Allen Brown for being the catalyst I needed to embark upon this journey. Without his encouragement, I probably would still be procrastinating.

I want to thank my siblings for just being there for me, loving and supporting me at times when I needed that support and did not feel lovable.

I want to thank Bishop William P. Wiggins Sr. and his wife Sis Lula Wiggins, Mother Eloise Goodman, Elder Thomas Wiggins Sr. and his wife Mother Jeanette Wiggins, and Ms. Ernestine Langston. To me, these beautiful Saints model what a Christian should be. They interacted with people based on biblical principles and not the status of the person.

I want to thank Elder Thomas Wiggins, who used to say, "Be careful what you do because you may be the only Bible some people ever read." Truer words were never spoken.

I want to thank these Saints of God, who were Bibles that I was reading, and no matter where God takes me in life, they will always be the faces on my Christian Mount Rushmore.

On August 13, 1992, I want to thank Bishop Wiggins, who called me to Christ in his office at New Mt. Joy.

I also want to thank Major Mays, chief of security at Deerfield Correction Center, for heeding the voice of the Holy Spirit and allowing God to show me through Him that He {God} was in my corner and that with God on my side, I had to win in life.

I also want to thank Chaplains Creach, Holms, and Chaplain Rob for being the right vessels at the right times in very difficult settings. You Guys are the best of the best.

I want to thank the Christian coalition. You Guys motivated me, pushed me, challenged me to be the best version of me that I could be. Together we touched and will touch a lot of lives for Jesus.

To my brothers at Deerfield — Rob Dull, Rob Morris, Step, Jessie, Bill, King, Rev., Brooks, Reggie, Giles, Dave — I really appreciate how much each of you were and are there for me.

I appreciate your willingness to encourage me when I was down and confront me when I was wrong. THANKS!

I want to thank Counselors Carr and Ludwig for really caring. You Guys are very special to me.

I want to thank Elder Gerald for being a great leader and teacher, for not just teaching but for being an example of what you teach and for your quest and hunger to grow and learn so you can continue to elevate your flock.

I want to thank my Wednesday night Bible study group: Minister Bond, Sis TT, Tinisha, Regina, Teddy, Sharon, Carolyn, and First Lady Goodman. You Guys motivate me.

In my darkest hours and loneliest moments, there were two people whom the thought of would give me the resolve to fight on and refuse any thoughts of quitting. I thank you for always being people that can motivate and challenge me. I am talking about my guy's Lil Randy and Deandre.

They say that we can accomplish anything in life if our why is big enough. You Guys are my WHY!

I have to thank two amazing women that have a special place and will always have a special place in my heart: Brittany and Shereen, my daughters-in-love, whom I met in a prison visiting room. I knew at once both of my boys had hit home runs.

I have to thank my motivation for wanting to make the world a better place. That motivation is Romel, Tres, Austin, and Rowan. I love you guys.

I want to thank my nieces and nephews for being the awesome people they are.

When I think of love and what the definition of love is, I do not see words. I see a person. That person is my soulmate. That person is my co-pilot on life's journey. That person is my wife of 48 years and more proof of the favor of God on my life. Love you, Annette.

Introduction

April 27, 1995, I'm sitting in my cell. I just woke up and I'm waiting to get dressed to head to the courtroom. Today, I'll be standing before the judge for sentencing on felony convictions. I don't know what to expect, but I do know what my lawyer has told me—he wants me to throw myself on the mercy of the court. I already told him I wasn't going to do that.

I wasn't going to beg for anyone's mercy, even though I took full responsibility for my situation and the choices that landed me here. There were things about the court process I felt had been wrong, and I wasn't going to ignore that. I had made my decision: I would face the judge and let him do what he had to do.

The deputies eventually came to get me. They escorted me to a holding cell in Suffolk City Jail in Virginia, where I waited until it was my turn to appear. Finally, the court called for me, and I was taken in to face my sentence.

When I saw my lawyer, he reiterated his advice to me, once again telling me to throw myself on the mercy of the court. I didn't respond. I just looked at him and said nothing.

Finally, I was standing before the judge. He asked if there was anything I wanted to say before sentencing. "Go ahead," he said. I told him that my lawyer had advised me to throw myself on the mercy of the court, but that I didn't agree with him.

I told the judge, "Even though I take full responsibility for the situation, I feel that there were things in this process that weren't handled right. I'm not going to stand here and beg for mercy. You do what you have to do. I'll overcome this."

The judge looked at me for a moment before he finally said, "You're a man who likes to be in control. But you're not in control anymore. The Commonwealth of Virginia is in control of your life now."

I looked him in the eyes and responded, "Your Honor, that may be true. But it's only temporary. I will regain control of my life."

The judge handed down his sentence: 100 years. One hundred years. Then he turned around and suspended 55 of those years, leaving me with a 45-year active sentence. He added that if I ever messed up, those 55 years could be reinstated.

When I left the courtroom and got back on the van heading to the jail, one of the other guys looked at me and asked, "What just happened in there?"

I told him exactly what I told you. He looked at me and said, "Man, I don't believe you."

"Why not?" I asked.

"Because you're too calm," he replied. "You just got sentenced to 45 active years with 55 hanging over your head and you're sitting here like it's nothing."

I looked at him and said, "I'm calm because I'm not focusing on the time. I'm focusing on what I need to do to overcome it. With God's help, I'm not going to let this time defeat me. I'm going to defeat it."

In that moment, I made a decision. I wasn't going to let this sentence define me. I wasn't going to let it break me. I didn't know how, but I knew that with God's help, I would make it through this.

And now, as you're reading this, I want you to know something: I don't know what you may be facing in your life. I don't know what kind of battles or challenges have been placed in your path. Maybe it's a health condition that the doctors have told you is hopeless. Maybe it's a financial crisis, a broken relationship, an addiction you've been struggling to break free from. Whatever it is, I'm here to tell you this: no matter how impossible it seems, you and God together can overcome it.

I'm not just saying this because it sounds good. I'm saying this because I've lived it. I know what it's like to face impossible circumstances. I know what it's like to feel like there's no way out. But I also know what can happen when you turn to God and work with Him. He will help you overcome any challenge, any battle, any situation you're facing.

This book is about my story—about how God stepped into my life and showed me that nothing is impossible with Him. Even before I was sentenced, God was already working in my life, warning me, trying to guide me. I didn't always see it at the time, but looking back, I can see His hand in every part of my journey.

My hope is that as you read this book, you'll find encouragement and strength for whatever you're facing. I hope it inspires you to turn to God and trust Him, because with Him on your side, there is no battle you can't win.

So buckle up and get ready, because this journey isn't just about me—it's about what God can do for you, too.

Chapter 1

Sentenced to 100 Years

God's Message About Prison Ministry

I'll never forget the moment when God spoke to me. I was praying, asking Him for deliverance, asking Him to bring me out. But His answer wasn't what I wanted to hear. God told me, "You're going to prison, and you're going to start your teaching ministry there."

When I heard that, my first reaction wasn't acceptance. I made light of it and thought to myself, Is there anybody else up there I can ask for an opinion? I didn't want to believe what I'd heard. I wasn't ready to hear it. But deep down, I knew it was Him speaking to me.

Looking back, it's clear now that God was preparing me for what was to come. But in that moment, I was resistant. I wasn't trying to hear that I was going to prison, let alone that my ministry would start there. I wrestled with it, trying to find another way, another answer. I just wasn't ready to accept it yet.

Initial Arrest and Coming Down from a High

When I first got arrested, I was coming down off a high. It took a few days for my mind to clear, and when it finally did, the reality of my situation started to hit me.

I remember sitting there, confused and overwhelmed, thinking to myself, *How did I get here?* It didn't make sense. I began to pray, asking God for clarity. I needed answers. *What happened? How did my life go so wrong? What did I do to end up in this place?*

I was searching for an explanation, something to help me make sense of the mess I'd made of my life. In those early days, I didn't fully understand what was happening. My mind was foggy, and I was wrestling with guilt, shame, and a thousand questions. But even in the midst of all that confusion, I found myself turning to God. I asked Him to show me where I went wrong and what I needed to do to change.

First Weeks in Prison – New Reality

After my sentencing, I spent about a month and a half in jail before they transported us to prison. That's when the reality of my situation really started to sink in. I didn't know what to expect—everything about this was new.

The day they told us to pack up, I remember getting on the bus with a group of other inmates. As we rode, I listened to the guys who

6

had been through this before, hearing their advice and what they thought was coming next. One of them told me we were headed to Powhatan Correctional Center, which, at the time, was considered one of the worst prisons in Virginia.

When we pulled up to Powhatan, another inmate on the bus turned to me and said, "This is the big house. Make sure you get a shank when you get in there." I looked at him, confused, and asked, "Why would I need that?" He just shook his head and said, "You'll see. You're gonna need it here. That's the way it is."

I wasn't afraid, but I didn't know what to expect either. It was like walking into a completely different world. I knew I had to figure out how to carry myself in this new environment, and I had to do it quickly.

That first night, I called home. I talked to my brother Reggie on the phone, and he told me, "You need to join the Nation of Islam. That way, you'll be protected." I told him, "I don't want or need that protection. I've got this." I wasn't about to rely on something like that.

The hardest part of adjusting wasn't fear; it was the loss of freedom. I had always been a free spirit, used to going where I wanted, when I wanted. Now, all of that was gone. Someone else decided when I got up, when I ate, and when I moved around. I was surrounded by people I didn't want to be around, and it was clear that my life was no longer my own.

At first, we were in what they called "receiving," which is where everyone goes when they first enter the prison system. It's separate from the general population, and they put you through a series of classes and evaluations to determine where you'll be placed.

Orientation and Prison Culture Shock

During orientation, they gave us a glimpse of what prison life was going to be like, but it also exposed the culture we were stepping into. The classes weren't just about the rules—they came with warnings about survival and situations that could arise.

One warning stuck out to me. The instructor told us, "If someone puts candy or cookies on your bed, don't touch it. If you take it, you're consenting to be their lover." He even gave a specific example, saying, "If someone puts a Snickers bar on your bed, don't take it."

I couldn't believe what I was hearing. The thought that something as small as candy could mean so much was shocking to me. I said, "I love Snickers. If someone puts a Snickers on my bed, I'm taking it—and that's going to be the end of that conversation." It made people laugh, but to me, the whole situation felt strange. It was hard to believe this was the kind of thing I needed to watch out for.

The guards were another story entirely. They didn't see us as people—they saw us as prisoners, and they treated us that way. During orientation, one of the guards asked, "Does anyone here have back problems?" I didn't raise my hand because I didn't have back problems. Then he asked, "Has anyone here ever had a back injury?" At that point, I raised my hand and said I had.

He immediately accused me of lying. "When I asked if you had back problems, you didn't raise your hand. But when I asked about back injuries, you did. That's a lie."

I stood my ground. "Listen to the questions you asked," I told him. "I don't have back problems, but I've had a back injury before. Those are two different things."

At the time, I didn't fully understand how serious a write-up could be or how it could affect things like my good time or parole eligibility. But I wasn't going to let them railroad me—not even on something as small as this.

The lessons during orientation were harsh, but they opened my eyes to the games, power struggles, and manipulation that existed in this new world. From that point forward, I made it my mission to remain disciplined, vigilant, and grounded—no matter what the system or its culture tried to throw at me.

Family Reactions to the Sentencing

The reactions from my family after my sentencing were hard to deal with, but they were also expected. Everyone responded differently, but one thing was clear—there was a lot of disappointment and hurt.

My sister Carolyn was one of the first people I spoke to after my incarceration. The first time I called her, she broke down crying on the phone. She said, "I hate where you are. I always thought you were smarter than the rest of us. I can't understand how you got to this point." Hearing her cry like that was painful, but I understood where she was coming from.

My mother's reaction was heartbreaking. When I called her, she cried, and I could hear how much this hurt her. She didn't say a lot, but her silence and her tears spoke volumes.

Even though my family loved me, I knew they couldn't fully understand what I was going through. I prayed they'd never have to experience the kind of addiction or situation that led me to this point, because it's something you can't fully explain to someone who hasn't lived it.

Buddy, my oldest brother, took it the hardest. He didn't say much to me at first, but later, when he came to visit, he told me, "I can't accept what you've done. I can't deal with this right now." Growing up, Buddy was the one I looked up to the most. I emulated him in so many ways. So when he told me he had to stay away, it really hit me.

Then there was my wife. Out of everyone, she was the one I hurt the most. We didn't talk for the entire first year of my incarceration. Not one phone call, not one letter. But she still brought our boys to see me. She'd bring DeAndre and Little Randy, and she'd also bring my mom. She didn't say a word to me during those visits, but she made sure my family came to see me.

I didn't hold anything against her—or any of them, for that matter. I knew I'd let them all down. I also knew they couldn't fully grasp what I was going through, and I prayed they'd never have to.

One moment that stuck out with me was when Michele, my niece, said something to me that I believe was from God. She told me, "If you do what you're supposed to do and get yourself back together, you'll get all your relationships back." Those words hit me deeply. It wasn't just her speaking—I felt like God was telling me something through her. From that moment on, I held onto her words. They gave me hope and a reminder that I needed to work on myself if I wanted to rebuild those relationships.

I made up my mind to fight through this, even if it meant doing it alone. I wasn't angry at my family for their reactions, because I understood their disappointment and pain. I knew I had to focus on me and figure out how to make things right, even though it would take time.

Internal Struggles and Determination to Change

When I first got to prison, I had a lot of time to sit with myself. The hardest part wasn't the bars or the loss of freedom it was looking at myself and realizing what I'd become. I felt disgusted. Disgusted that I'd let my life spiral to the point where I was in this situation. I kept asking myself, *How did I get here?*

In the beginning, I wrestled with the weight of my choices. It wasn't just the physical reality of being locked up; it was the realization that I had destroyed the life I once had. I had let my addiction and bad decisions take me down a road that I never thought I'd travel. I was disappointed in myself and overwhelmed by guilt for what I'd done to the people who loved me.

At the same time, I knew sitting in that guilt wasn't going to get me anywhere. I had to make a decision: either let this break me, or figure out how to change. I decided I wasn't going to let prison define who I was. I wasn't going to let it win.

I started turning inward and focusing on me. I began to think about the kind of man I wanted to be, not just in prison, but after I got out. I prayed and asked God to help me figure it out. *What do I need to learn from this? How do I move forward from here? What can I do to become better?* These were the questions I asked myself every day.

I knew it wasn't going to be easy, but I also knew I had no choice. I couldn't change the fact that I was here, but I could change how I responded to it. I made a decision to use this time to grow, to become the man I knew I could be.

It wasn't just about surviving prison—it was about transforming my mind and my spirit. I started paying attention to the things I needed to work on within myself. I focused on developing a mindset that wasn't tied to the walls around me, but to the future I wanted to create.

Even though I felt disgusted with where I was, I also felt a growing determination. I wasn't going to let this be the end of my story. I wasn't going to let my horrible choices define me.

Final Reflection on the Early Prison Experience

In the early days, as I wrestled with my new reality, I started thinking more deeply about spiritual warfare. I didn't fully understand it at first, but I felt like I was in the middle of it. There was this constant pull, a battle between giving in to despair and holding on to hope. I knew I needed to pray, but I didn't just want to pray—I wanted to understand what prayer really meant.

I started asking God to teach me. I prayed for clarity, for strength, and for wisdom. As I began studying prayer and righteousness, I started to see things differently. Prayer wasn't just about asking for things or hoping for answers—it was about aligning myself with God's will. Righteousness wasn't just about doing the right thing; it was about living on the outside what the grace of God had made me on the inside.

These lessons weren't easy. I had to face a lot of hard truths about myself and my choices. But through it all, I felt like God was guiding me, showing me how to grow and prepare for something greater. I didn't know what that was yet, but I knew I had to trust Him.

By resisting the prison mentality and focusing on spiritual growth, I started to feel a sense of purpose. I wasn't just surviving—I was transforming. And that's what kept me going.

Chapter 1: Reflection Section: Lessons to Take Away

Let me share some lessons from my own journey that I believe will resonate with you and help you grow:

- **God's Plan May Be Uncomfortable but Necessary:** I didn't want to accept that God had a purpose for me in prison. It challenged everything I thought I wanted. But I've learned that when God's plan feels uncomfortable, it's often because it's exactly what we need for transformation. Trust Him—He knows what He's doing.
- **The Pain of Accountability:** One of the hardest parts of my journey was facing the disappointment of people I loved. I had to own my actions, even when it hurt. But taking that accountability opened the door to healing and rebuilding trust.
- **The Importance of Self-Reflection:** Prison forced me to look in the mirror and confront my choices. Instead of getting stuck in guilt or bitterness, I used that time to grow. Self-reflection is one of the most powerful tools for transformation.
- **Spiritual Warfare is Real:** I faced a battle between despair and hope. It wasn't just emotional—it was spiritual. Prayer and focusing on God became my anchor in the storm. Trust me, aligning with Him will carry you through your toughest battles.
- **Transformation Starts in the Mind:** I made a choice not to get stuck in a "prison mentality." Instead, I focused on who I wanted to become. Your mindset is the key to breaking free from any adversity.

Action Steps for You

Let's apply these lessons to your life:

- **Reflect on a Current Challenge:** Are you resisting something God may be using to grow or prepare you? Take a moment to pray and ask for clarity, then trust His plan.
- **Take Ownership:** Is there a part of your life where you need to step up and take responsibility? Make amends if necessary, and commit to growing from the experience.
- **Resist a Negative Mentality:** Are you letting your circumstances define who you are? Start visualizing the person you want to become, and take steps to align your life with that vision.
- **Strengthen Your Prayer Life:** When you pray, focus on more than outcomes. Ask God for wisdom and guidance, and let Him shape your journey.

Insights for Prayer

Here are some things I've found helpful in prayer that I believe can guide you too:

- **Prayer Focus:** Ask God to reveal the purpose behind what you're facing. Pray for the strength to embrace the growth He's calling you to.
- **Meditation Scripture:** Spend time reflecting on Proverbs 29:18: "Where there is no vision, the people perish, but happy is he who keeps the law."
- **Pray for Righteousness:** Ask God to help you become the person He created you to be, aligning your thoughts and actions with His will.

Visualize Your Transformation: Take a few minutes each day to picture the person you'll become as you follow God's guidance. Let that vision inspire your faith and drive your actions.

Chapter 1 Sentenced to 100 Years

Prompt: Write one or more goals for how you can respond to overwhelming challenges with faith and courage. Include a prayer outline to guide your thoughts, which you can revisit later for reflection.

_____

_____

_____

_____

_____

_____

_____

_____

_____

_____

_____

_____

_____

_____

_____

_____

_____

_____

_____

_____

_____

_____

Chapter 2

How Did I Get Here?

Upbringing and Family Life

Growing up as the 10th sibling in a family of 11 kids was an experience I'll always cherish. My older brothers and sisters were incredible. They set examples for me and my younger brother Reggie that I'll never forget. I've always said I had the best older siblings in the world because of how much they did for us. They took care of us, looked out for us, and made sure we had what we needed.

We grew up in Suffolk, Virginia, in a close-knit family. Life wasn't always easy, but we had each other, and that meant everything. My siblings weren't just role models—they were a source of support and inspiration. They showed me what it meant to work hard, to care for family, and to be there for one another.

I was active as a kid, always playing sports. I played basketball, baseball, and just about anything else I could. I loved being on the court or the field, and sports became a big part of my life. Looking back, I think about how different things could have been if my parents had let me play football.

When I was in the eighth grade, I broke a finger playing football. After that, my parents decided I wasn't allowed to play anymore. They told me, "No more football—focus on basketball." At the time, I was disappointed, but I listened to them. By the time I got to my senior year of high school, they finally said, "If you want to, you can play football now." But by then, I was already doing so well on the basketball court that I didn't want to go back to football.

Even as a teenager, I wasn't like a lot of the kids I went to school with. I didn't drink or get into trouble. My peers used to joke with me, saying, "When we're older, you'll be the one sitting around with a Pepsi while the rest of us are having a drink." And they were probably right. Drinking just wasn't something I was into.

The influence of my family and the lessons I learned from them shaped who I was during those early years. My upbringing gave me a foundation of discipline and determination, and sports gave me an outlet to focus my energy and dreams. Those years were some of the best of my life, and I'll always be grateful for the family that supported me and the opportunities I had growing up.

School Years and College Experience

After graduating from high school, I earned a basketball scholarship and headed off to college. In the beginning, basketball was my whole focus. I spent so much time practicing and playing that I didn't really experience college life the way most people do. My first two years were all about the game—I was tied up in basketball and didn't really see anything else outside of it.

Then, I ended up redshirting, which meant I had to sit out for a year. That year changed my perspective entirely. For the first time, I got to see college in a different light. Without basketball, I realized how much more there was to life at school. I started to enjoy college for what it was, not just as a platform for basketball. In fact, I enjoyed it so much that when my redshirt year was over, I didn't want to go back to playing. My priorities had shifted, and I no longer felt like basketball was what I wanted to focus on.

At that point, I was married and still in school, but I was also starting to feel the weight of needing to support my family. I was only about a year away from graduating when I decided to leave school and get a job. Looking back, it's a decision I regret sometimes, but in the moment, I felt like it was the right thing to do for my family.

Working at the Shipyard

After leaving college, I got a job at the Newport News Shipyard. In Suffolk, Virginia, where I grew up, the shipyard was considered one of the best places to work. If you got a Job with the Navy Naval

21

Shipyard, Newport News Shipyard or Lipton Tea you were seen as having a stable and respectable career. But even though the shipyard was considered a great opportunity, I didn't like it much when I first got there.

I started on the night shift, which made the adjustment even harder. The work wasn't something I was passionate about, and I found myself questioning if this was really what I wanted to do. Then, I was approached by someone who introduced me to the apprenticeship program. He told me about the program's benefits and explained that it was essentially a fast track to management positions.

At first, I wasn't interested. I had left basketball behind and thought my days of trying to climb any kind of ladder were over. But after doing some research, I realized that if I was going to stay at the shipyard, the apprenticeship program might give me more opportunities down the line. So, I decided to join.

Once I entered the program, I faced challenges that I hadn't expected. Early on, I encountered a craft instructor who was openly discriminatory. I'll never forget how he treated me. After my first quarter in the program, I failed algebra because I had been goofing off and not taking things seriously. This instructor saw that F as an opportunity to put me down. He said to me, "We're going to butt heads, and you're probably going to fail."

I was taken aback, but at the same time, I made a silent promise to myself. I was going to prove him wrong. He wasn't just critical—

he was openly disrespectful, and it was clear that race played a role in how he treated me. He doubted my ability to succeed and wasn't shy about letting me know it. But instead of letting his words discourage me, I used them as fuel.

I told myself, *I'm going to make it through this program. I'm going to prove him wrong and watch him eat every word he said.* I knew I had been slacking in that first quarter, but I also knew that I was capable of doing better. I buckled down and pushed myself to succeed, not just to earn the certificate at the end of the program, but to show that no one could dictate my potential.

The apprenticeship program became more than just a path to management—it became a personal challenge. I stayed focused, worked hard, and made it through, despite the obstacles. Looking back, I realize that instructor's doubt and prejudice only made me more determined to prove what I was capable of achieving.

Introduction to Drugs and Addiction

My introduction to drugs happened while I was working at the shipyard. At first, I didn't see it coming. I had a coworker I got close to, and one day, he told me, "Man, you know what I do to get through the day? I get high." He said it casually, like it was no big deal, and then he added, "You should try it too."

At first, I wasn't sure what to think, but he made it sound so normal. He said, "Look, you'll feel better. It'll make the day go by easier." Eventually, I started doing it with him. I began smoking marijuana and trying cocaine. At the time, I didn't think much of it. It was just a way to relax and escape the pressures of the job.

What started off as an occasional thing quickly turned into a habit. It didn't take long before we were doing it all the time. One day, my coworker said, "You know, we're spending a lot of money on this. Why not sell it and use that money to pay for what we do?" I thought it was a good idea at the time, so I went along with it.

I'll never forget the first time I tried cocaine. We were at a friend's house in Suffolk, and everyone was getting high. I remember sitting there, watching them, and thinking, *I'm never going to do that. Look at how they're acting—why would anyone want to feel like that?* But that night, something changed. I told myself, *Let me just try it once.*

The moment I tried it, I was hooked. From that very first time, it had me. I didn't even realize how fast it was taking control of my life. Before I knew it, I was making decisions based on drugs. Everything I did was centered around getting high. I started spending all my money on it, even though I was making good money at the shipyard. It didn't matter how much I was earning—every cent was going toward feeding my addiction.

That decision to try cocaine for the first time was the beginning of a downward spiral. It changed the way I thought, the way I acted, and the way I lived. It wasn't just a habit anymore—it became my life.

Spiritual Ignorance and Challenges

When I look back, I can see how spiritually ignorant I was. At the time, I didn't even realize what I was up against. I was walking blind, thinking I was in control, when in reality, I was being led down a path I couldn't see. I didn't understand anything about spiritual warfare or the way the enemy works to deceive us.

One of the biggest mistakes I ever made happened before I even understood the weight of what I was doing. I remember talking to some guys one day, and I said something that I now know was incredibly foolish. I told Satan, "I challenge you. I'll take you on. You can't beat me. I can handle you."

That was the dumbest thing I ever said. I had no idea what I was dealing with or who I was up against. I was walking around like I had everything under control, but I didn't. I wasn't prepared for the spiritual fight I was stepping into, and I lost that battle badly.

Later, I began to understand the implications of what I had said and done. There's a passage in the Bible where the Apostle Paul says, "We are not ignorant of his devices." At the time, I didn't understand what that meant. I didn't realize that Satan doesn't need to force us into anything. He's cunning, and he knows how to lead us down the wrong path without us even realizing it.

Another scripture in 2 Corinthians 10:5 talks about "casting down imaginations" and "taking every thought captive to the obedience of Christ." What's interesting is that the word "thoughts" in that verse and the word "devices" in the other passage both come from the same Greek word. It's about a mindset—the way we think and the meaning we attach to our thoughts.

At the time, I didn't understand any of this. I didn't know I was being deceived, and I didn't recognize the traps that were being laid out for me. I thought I was in control, but in reality, I was being led like a lamb to the slaughter.

It wasn't until I was in the middle of the fire that I started to realize what was happening. I had to face the truth that as smart as I thought I was, I was completely ignorant spiritually. I didn't understand what I was fighting, and that ignorance left me wide open to attack. We are no match for satan on our own.

Chapter 2: Reflection and Insights: Lessons to Take Away

Here are some key lessons from my journey that I hope will inspire and challenge you:

- **The Strength of Family Foundations:** My upbringing taught me the value of strong family relationships. Those early lessons shaped my character and gave me strength when times got tough. Think about the role your family—or your chosen family—plays in shaping who you are.
- **Resilience in the Face of Opposition:** I faced discrimination and challenges early in life, but I chose to persevere. It wasn't easy, but faith and determination helped me overcome. You can do the same when you lean on God and trust His promises.
- **The Danger of Small Compromises:** My introduction to drugs didn't start with big decisions—it began with small, seemingly harmless choices. I encourage you to evaluate your own life and be mindful of the small decisions that can lead to significant consequences.
- **Spiritual Awareness is Key:** I didn't recognize the enemy's tactics early on, and it left me vulnerable. Understanding God's truth and equipping yourself spiritually will guard you against deception.
- **God's Redemption Through Reflection:** Even in my failures, God was at work. He used those moments to teach me and help me grow. Take heart—your story is still being written, and God can redeem every part of it.

Action Steps for You

Let's put these lessons into action in your own life:

- **Reflect on Your Choices:** Are there small compromises in your life that could lead you away from God's plan? Take time to pray and ask Him for the strength to correct your course.

- **Overcome Adversity with Faith:** When challenges arise, don't give up. Lean on God's promises and trust that He is working everything for your good.
- **Seek Spiritual Understanding:** Spend time in God's Word to grow spiritually and guard your mind. Use scriptures like 2 Corinthians 10:5 to take every thought captive to Christ.
- **Commit to Growth:** Ask God to reveal areas where He wants you to grow. Be intentional about taking the steps He shows you.

Insights for Prayer

Here are some things you can pray about as you reflect on this chapter:

- **Pray for Guidance:** Ask God to reveal any areas of compromise in your life and give you the wisdom to make better choices.
- **Seek Strength for Resilience:** Pray for the strength to endure adversity and remain steadfast in your faith.
- **Ask for Spiritual Discernment:** Pray for the ability to recognize the enemy's traps and to align your thoughts with God's truth.
- **Thank God for Redemption:** Take time to thank Him for His grace and His ability to restore and transform, no matter where you've been.

Chapter 2 How Did I Get Here?

Prompt: Write one or more actions to take responsibility for your life and make positive changes. Include a prayer asking for clarity and strength to move forward

_____

_____

_____

_____

_____

_____

_____

_____

_____

_____

_____

_____

_____

_____

_____

_____

_____

_____

_____

_____

Chapter 3

The Grip of Addiction

Escalation of Addiction

Once cocaine got a hold of me, it didn't let go. My life quickly spiraled out of control. Every decision I made revolved around getting high, and nothing else mattered. It was like my logic, my values, and everything I once cared about disappeared.

My addiction didn't just affect me—it consumed my marriage, my family, and everything I was supposed to be. I started taking money from my wife's purse, money I knew we needed for groceries or to take care of our kids, and I spent it on drugs. I didn't do it once or twice—I did it more times than I care to admit. Looking back, I can't believe I was capable of doing something like that. How could I betray my family like that? But in the moment, the addiction was stronger than anything else.

There were also nights when I found myself lying on the floor, crying and begging God to take me out of this world. I was so desperate—so trapped in this cycle of addiction—that I didn't see any other way out. I would cry out to God, "Please deliver me from this, or just take me out of here because I can't do this anymore." I hated the person I had become, but I felt completely powerless to change it.

At one point, I even checked myself into one of the best drug rehab programs in the country. It was known as one of the top two places in America for addiction recovery, and I went in hoping they could help me. But when I got there, I saw people who had been through the program three or four times. That broke me. I thought, *If they can't break free, what hope do I have?* Instead of feeling motivated, I felt defeated, like I was trapped in something I could never escape.

Through it all, my wife tried to stay strong. She was a trooper—she stood by me longer than anyone else would have. But even she had her breaking point. Addiction doesn't just destroy the addict—it destroys the people who love them. I put her through so much pain, and even though she tried to support me, there was only so much she could take.

My addiction took everything from me—my marriage, my self-respect, and my ability to think clearly. It turned me into someone I didn't recognize. My life wasn't my own anymore. Every decision I made was dictated by the drugs, and it tore everything apart.

Reckless and Dangerous Actions

The addiction didn't just affect my family—it pushed me into reckless and dangerous situations that could've easily cost me my life. I started doing things that I would've never imagined, and the scariest part was that I didn't even care.

One of the most foolish things I did was take drugs from dealers without paying for them. I would take what I wanted, and the next day, I'd go right back to the same dealers as if nothing had happened. I didn't try to hide or avoid them. I'd stand there laughing and joking, like it was all just a game. Looking back, I can't believe how reckless that was. These weren't people to mess with—any one of them could've killed me on the spot, but I didn't think about that at the time.

I also made dangerous choices with my car. I started letting dealers borrow it in exchange for drugs. I knew full well they could use it for anything—selling drugs, committing crimes, or even taking it and never bringing it back. But in my mind, all that mattered was that I got what I wanted. I didn't care about the risk, and I didn't think about the consequences.

I put myself in dangerous situations without a second thought. I would go to some of the roughest neighborhoods at all hours of the night, completely ignoring the risks. I was walking into places where anything could happen—places where people got robbed, shot, or worse—and I didn't care. The addiction had me so blinded that nothing else mattered.

Recognizing Addiction's Power

Cocaine has a power that's hard to put into words. From the very first time I tried it, it had a hold on me. I didn't realize how addictive it was until it was too late. At first, it seemed harmless. I thought it was just a way to relax, to let off some steam. But before long, it took over my mind, my actions, and my life.

One of the things about cocaine is that it tricks you. The first time you use it, you feel this incredible high—this rush that makes you think nothing in the world can touch you. But what it doesn't tell you is that you'll spend every moment after that chasing that same high, and you'll almost never feel it again. It's like the proverbial ghost. You keep going after something that you can't really catch, but you don't stop trying.

Cocaine didn't just affect the way I felt—it consumed my thoughts. Everything I did revolved around it. My mind was constantly calculating: *When can I get it? How can I get it? How much do I need?* It wasn't about living my life anymore. It was about feeding the addiction. My every thought and decision was shaped by it.

I started making excuses for my behavior, convincing myself that I was still in control. I'd say things like, "I can stop whenever I want," or, "It's just something I'm doing to get through a tough time." But the truth was, I wasn't in control. The addiction was. It had its grip on me, and no matter how hard I tried to convince myself otherwise, I was powerless against it.

Addiction doesn't just ruin your body; it takes over your mind. It becomes this constant voice in your head, always pushing you to do whatever it takes to keep it satisfied. It doesn't care about your family, your future, or your well-being. It just keeps pulling you deeper and deeper, until you can't see a way out.

For me, cocaine wasn't just a drug—it was a master. It controlled me in ways I never thought possible. And the scariest part was how it all felt so normal while I was in it. It wasn't until I started reflecting on the damage it had done that I realized just how much power it had over me.

Impact on Relationships

My addiction didn't just affect me—it hurt the people I cared about the most. My wife, my kids, and my family all felt the weight of my choices, even though they weren't the ones making them. The strain it put on my marriage was something I'll never forget, and the guilt of what I put my boys through still lingers in my mind.

My wife was a fighter. She tried her best to stick by me and support me through everything. She stayed longer than most people would have. But even the strongest person has a breaking point. Addiction doesn't just break the person who's using—it breaks everyone around them. It tears apart trust, love, and connection. And it did just that in my marriage.

I know there were times when my wife didn't understand what I was going through, and to be honest, I didn't understand it myself. I couldn't explain why I kept going back to the drugs or why I couldn't just stop, even though I wanted to. She was there, trying to help, but I kept pushing her further and further away.

Then there were my boys. I missed out on so much of their lives because I was too caught up in my addiction. I wasn't there for them the way a father should be. I didn't get to see them grow up the way I wanted to, and that's a regret I'll carry forever.

When I think back to those years, the thing that hits me the hardest is the lost time. You can't get that back. I missed birthdays, moments, and milestones. I wasn't the father they needed, and I wasn't the husband my wife deserved.

The addiction didn't just steal from me—it stole from them, too. And that's something I'll always have to live with.

Missed Career Opportunities

One of the greatest opportunities I lost because of my addiction was with Dale Carnegie. It was something I had spoken into existence—I used to tell people, "I'm going to work for them one day." I truly believed it, and I kept saying it over and over, almost like I was willing it to happen.

Then, one day, my wife came to me with an ad she found in the paper. She said, "Randy, look—Dale Carnegie is hiring." After all the times I had spoken about it, here was the opportunity right in front of me.

I called them immediately, and they told me about a group interview happening in Virginia Beach. When I got there, I saw about 100 people in the room, all competing for just six positions.

They explained that we'd each have to record a three-minute video explaining why we should be chosen. After a short break, only about 20 of us returned to complete the challenge, and I was one of them.

The very next day, I got a call saying they wanted me to come back for a second interview. Out of the remaining group of about 10 or 12, I made it to the final six. The people at Dale Carnegie saw potential in me, and they even talked about how far I could go with the company. They said I might even be able to own my own franchise someday.

But no matter how much potential they saw in me, the addiction wouldn't let me succeed. I completed the training and took the classes, but after a few months, I walked away.

At the time, I told myself I left because I had gotten what I needed from the experience. But the truth is, the addiction wouldn't let me move forward. It kept pulling me back, and I wasn't in a place where I could fully embrace the opportunity.

Dale Carnegie could've been life-changing. It could've set me on a path to something incredible, but I let it slip through my fingers. It's one of my biggest regrets, knowing how much that opportunity could've meant for me and my family.

Desperation and Pivotal Moments

At the height of my addiction, I reached a point of pure desperation. I hated what the drugs had done to me, and I hated the power they had over my life. But instead of focusing that hatred on the addiction itself, I started to focus it on the people I blamed for feeding it: the drug dealers.

I remember thinking to myself, *If I can't beat the addiction, maybe I can destroy the people who are pushing it.* I got to a place where I seriously considered arming myself and going after the drug dealers in my community. My plan was simple—see how many I could take out before I got caught.

That's how deep into despair I was. I wasn't thinking about the consequences or the damage it would cause. All I could see was the anger and frustration I felt toward the drugs and the people supplying them. At the time, it felt like the only way I could fight back.

Looking back now, I realize how dangerous that mindset was. If I had gone through with that plan, I wouldn't be here today. I wouldn't have survived it. It's only by God's grace that I didn't take that path, but at the time, I didn't see any other way out.

In a strange way, going to prison saved me. It stopped me from making decisions that could've ruined my life even further. It forced me to sit still and face the reality of where I was and what I had become. If I had not gone to prison when I did, I might not be alive today.

Prison didn't feel like salvation at the time, but now I can see how it was part of God's plan to pull me out of the chaos. It gave me a chance to stop running, to stop sinking deeper into the addiction, and to find a way to turn my life around.

That moment of desperation—when I was ready to take up arms against drug dealers—was a turning point for me. It showed me just how far I had fallen and how badly I needed help. And while it might seem strange to say, prison became the place where I finally started to see a glimmer of hope.

Chapter 3: Reflection Section: Lessons to Take Away

Here are some lessons from my journey that I want to share with you:

- **Addiction's Devastation:** Addiction doesn't just harm the person caught in it—it tears apart families, damages relationships, and steals opportunities. I've seen its destruction firsthand, and I want to encourage you to take a hard look at how it's affecting your life or someone you love.
- **The Danger of Reckless Choices:** Addiction has a way of making us feel invincible, but that false confidence leads to life-threatening decisions. I've been there, and I know how easy it is to overlook the risks.
- **Power of Self-Deception:** Addiction clouds judgment. It convinces you that harmful actions are justifiable. But I'm here to tell you—what seems normal in addiction is often anything but.
- **Missed Potential is a Warning:** I let opportunities slip through my fingers because addiction distracted me from my goals. Don't let that happen to you—stay focused and committed to the path God has for you.
- **God's Interventions Through Hardship:** Sometimes, the very thing you resist, like the hardships I faced in prison, becomes the turning point for your life. God can use those moments to change everything.

Action Steps for You

Let's take what we've learned and turn it into action:

- **Acknowledge the Grip of Addiction:** If you're struggling with addiction or know someone who is, take time to identify where it's taken hold. Commit to seeking help and asking God for deliverance.

- **Reflect on Reckless Decisions:** Are there choices you've made recently that are putting you or others at risk? Pray for clarity to see the dangers and take steps to correct your path.
- **Pursue Healing Relationships:** Think about someone whose trust you've broken. Take a step this week—whether it's having an honest conversation, apologizing, or starting counseling—to rebuild that connection.
- **Recognize God's Hand in Hardship:** Look back at a difficult time in your life and ask God to show you how He was working through it to grow you or prepare you for something greater.

Insights for Prayer

Here are some areas to focus on in prayer this week:

- **Pray for Deliverance:** Ask God to break the chains of addiction for yourself or someone close to you. Remember, He is stronger than any struggle.
- **Seek God's Guidance in Hard Times:** Pray for the strength to trust God's plan, even when you're going through hardship. Ask Him to reveal His purpose in your pain.
- **Ask for Restoration:** Bring broken relationships to God. Pray for His help in healing wounds and restoring trust.
- **Thank God for His Grace:** Reflect on how God's grace has protected you, even in your mistakes, and express your gratitude for His mercy.

Chapter 3 The Grip of Addiction

Prompt: Reflect on areas of your life where addiction—whether physical, emotional, or spiritual—may have taken hold. Write one or more goals for breaking free and include a prayer for strength and guidance.

_____

_____

_____

_____

_____

_____

_____

_____

_____

_____

_____

_____

_____

_____

_____

_____

_____

_____

_____

_____

_____

_____

_____

_____

Chapter 4

Rejecting God and Christianity

Early Rejection of Christianity

I was raised in a loving home with two incredible parents, Marjorie, and Norman White. They believed in Christian values and made sure that me and my siblings grew up in the church. It wasn't an option for us—if it was Sunday, we were going to church. In our house, the rule was simple: if you didn't go to church, you weren't going anywhere else that day.

Even though my parents made us attend church, it didn't mean I embraced it wholeheartedly. As I got older, I started to notice things that didn't sit right with me. When I was at church, I'd hear certain things being preached, but what I saw in people's lives didn't match up. The contradictions I witnessed between what was being taught and what was being lived made me question everything.

One of the scriptures I couldn't stand to hear growing up was Romans 8:28: *"And we know that all things work together for good to them that love God, to them who are the called according to his purpose."* I disliked it because, in my experience, it always seemed to be quoted after something terrible had happened.

People would use that verse to say, "This is going to work together for good," but as a kid, I couldn't understand how that could be true. If someone had just suffered a tragic loss, what good could possibly come out of that for them? I struggled to wrap my mind around the idea, and instead of comforting me, the verse made me angry. I later found out that Romans 8:28 is not a stand alone verse, verses 26 and 27 must be included to get the true meaning, yet never did I hear anyone include those verses when discussing Romans 8:28.

The Book of Job was another part of the Bible I wanted nothing to do with. If I went to church and the preacher started talking about Job, I'd check out immediately. I didn't even want to hear it. The story of Job scared me—it made me think that God was cruel. Here was a man who was faithful, upright, and devoted to God, yet God allowed him to lose everything. For what? To prove a point to Satan?

I couldn't reconcile the idea of a loving God with what Job went through. It seemed like God would do anything to bring Himself glory, even if it meant putting someone like Job through unimaginable suffering. I remember saying to myself, *If this is who God is, I can't serve Him.*

Even though people would talk about how Job was blessed in the end, all I could think about was the pain and loss he endured. Sure, God restored him and gave him more than he had before, but what about the people Job lost? They weren't brought back. The children he buried didn't return. That part of the story always stuck with me, and I couldn't get past it.

As I sat in church and heard people talk about God being a healer, I looked around and saw people who were sick and suffering. They'd talk about God as a provider, but I'd see people struggling and barely getting by. None of it made sense to me, and the more I thought about it, the angrier I became.

By the time I was old enough to make my own decisions, I couldn't wait to tell my parents I wasn't going to church anymore. I was done. I didn't accept God, and I certainly didn't accept Christianity.

First Rejection and Turning to New Age

The first time I truly rejected Christianity came when I was in college. By then, I had already walked away from the church I grew up in, and I wasn't interested in going back. I couldn't reconcile the things I'd experienced and heard in church with what I saw in the real world. So, I told myself I was done with it.

But one day, while I was sitting on the waterfront at Hampton University, I had an epiphany. I was just relaxing, watching the water, when I saw a seagull dive down and catch a fish. In that moment, it hit me—how could the seagull even know that fish was

47

there? It seemed impossible. The more I thought about it, the more I realized there was no way something like that could happen by chance. There had to be something bigger behind it.

That experience opened my eyes to the reality of God. For the first time, I truly believed He existed. But just because I accepted the existence of God didn't mean I accepted Christianity. I still had a lot of doubts, and I didn't think Christianity had all the answers.

I started to believe that religion was largely shaped by where you were born and how you were raised. If you were born in the United States, you'd probably grow up Christian. If you were born in the Middle East, you'd likely grow up Muslim. It all felt like chance, and I didn't think one belief system could be the ultimate truth.

So instead of going back to Christianity, I turned to New Age teachings. At the time, New Age spirituality seemed to make sense to me. It was practical, and a lot of the ideas felt like they worked in my life. I started reading books on New Age philosophies, studying their principles, and practicing what they taught.

But as I went deeper into New Age practices, I noticed something that surprised me. Almost every New Age book I read kept referencing Jesus. They'd talk about His teachings, His principles, and His life. It confused me at first—I thought I had walked away from Christianity, but here I was, constantly coming across Jesus in these New Age texts.

That curiosity led me to pick up the Bible for the first time in my life, not just to read it, but to study it. I wanted to see for myself what it said and how it connected to the ideas I was encountering in New Age spirituality. What I found shocked me.

As I studied the Bible, I realized that many of the principles and spiritual laws I had embraced in New Age teachings were already there, written in Scripture all along. It was like the truths I had been searching for outside of Christianity were in the Bible the entire time—I just hadn't seen them before.

It was through this process of studying the Bible that I came back to Christianity. The more I read, the more I saw that the answers I was looking for were there. It wasn't about religion anymore—it was about understanding God's word and His truth.

Second Rejection After Seeking Help for Addiction

The second time I rejected Christianity came after I joined a church and sought help for my addiction. At that point, I was struggling with drugs, and I knew I needed help. I decided to attend a Bible study one Tuesday night, hoping the church could guide me and help me find a way to break free.

I remember walking in and telling them, "I need help to get free from this drug addiction." I was vulnerable, laying it all out there, expecting compassion and guidance. But instead of offering support, one of the prominent sisters in the church said something that completely shattered my hope.

She looked at me and said, "Your problem is simple—just stop sinning."

The way she said it wasn't just dismissive—it was arrogant and condescending. It wasn't just the words she said, but the tone, the lack of understanding, the complete disregard for the struggle I was going through. In that moment, it felt like I had come to the church for help and been completely turned away.

I knew what my problem was. I didn't need someone to tell me I was sinning—I already knew that. What I needed was someone to help me, to guide me out of the darkness I was in. But instead, I was met with judgment and a lack of compassion.

That was the final straw for me. I decided I wanted nothing more to do with Christianity. I told myself it was a bunch of garbage and walked away from the church.

The decision to leave wasn't something I made lightly. Before this moment, I had been given a vision—a clear warning from God—not to leave the church. In the vision, God showed me the dangers of walking away, but at the time, I ignored it. I let my frustration and bitterness take over, and I left anyway.

Looking back, I can see now that the person in that church didn't turn me away because She didn't want to help. She turned me away because She didn't know how to help. But in the moment, it didn't feel that way. It felt like rejection, and it pushed me further away from God.

Leaving the church after that incident was one of the biggest mistakes I've ever made. God had warned me not to leave, but I didn't listen. Instead, I let my anger and disappointment drive my decisions, and it opened the door to even more struggles in my life.

Visions and Dreams: God's Warnings

One of the most vivid ways God has communicated with me throughout my life has been through dreams. These weren't just ordinary dreams—they were warnings, messages meant to guide and protect me. But there were times when I didn't fully understand what they meant, and other times when I ignored them altogether.

The first dream I'll never forget was about a Black Horse. I was at my mother's house, out in the area where we grew up, and I decided to walk to the store. The store was a little over half a mile away, so I made my way there, but on my way back, something happened.

As I walked home, I was suddenly chased by a Black Horse. It came after me full force, and I ran as fast as I could. The horse chased me all the way to the steps of the church I was attending at the time, New Gospel Temple. The steps to the church were about six or seven feet from the road, and I ran straight up them, trying to get inside.

When I turned around, the horse was standing there at the bottom of the steps. That's when I realized the horse wouldn't—or couldn't—come onto the church grounds. It stopped right there, unable to take another step forward.

At that moment, I started taunting the horse. I yelled at it, "You can't get me now! You can't come up here! You can't touch me as long as I'm on the church grounds!"

But then something happened that I wasn't expecting. The horse spoke to me. It said, "No, I can't get you as long as you stay on the church grounds. But if you come out, I'll get you."

When I woke up, the dream felt strange and unsettling, but I didn't fully understand its meaning at the time. It wasn't until much later that I realized God was warning me. He knew I was going to go to that church and ask for help, and He also knew they wouldn't give me the support I needed. But the warning was clear: no matter what happens, don't leave the church.

Unfortunately, I didn't listen. When I left the church after being turned away, I opened myself up to spiritual attacks. The Black Horse in the dream was Satan, and by leaving the church, I left the protection God had given me.

Around the same time, my wife had a dream of her own. She dreamed that we were at my mother's house, in the backyard. In the dream, there were demons all around us, trying to get to us, but they couldn't cross a certain line. There were two lambs walking around, and the demons couldn't get past them.

To this day, I believe those lambs represented Christ, the Lamb of God, protecting me and my family. My wife said that in the dream, the lambs were shielding us from the demons, keeping them at bay. Even now, I don't fully understand why there were two lambs instead of one, but what I do know is that God was showing us His protection.

Both of those dreams were warnings. God was telling me to stay close to Him, to stay under His protection, and not to leave the place He had directed me to. But I didn't heed the warning, and I paid the price for it.

When I left the church, I allowed myself to become vulnerable to spiritual attacks. It wasn't that God abandoned me—I abandoned Him. I stepped outside of His covering, and that's when the enemy took his chance to come after me.

Looking back, I can see the lessons in those dreams. God is always trying to guide us and protect us, but we have to be willing to listen. Sometimes the warnings are subtle, and sometimes they're loud and clear, like they were for me. But if we ignore them, we open ourselves up to danger.

Chapter 4: Reflection Section: Lessons to Take Away

Here's what I want you to take away from this chapter and how it can speak to your journey:

- **Rejection of Faith Often Stems from Hurt:** Like me, maybe you've turned away from God or the church because of disappointment or hurt. I rejected Christianity because I saw hypocrisy and a lack of compassion. But God wants us to know that His love is perfect, even when His people fall short.
- **God's Pursuit is Relentless:** When I sought answers in New Age teachings, God still found ways to draw me back to Him. He never gives up on us, and He's always reaching out, no matter where we are.
- **Warnings from God Must Be Heeded:** Dreams and visions aren't just coincidences. God uses them to protect and guide us. When I ignored His warnings, I faced unnecessary struggles.
- **Churches Need to Be Equipped to Help:** My experiences showed me how much we need churches to be places of understanding and support, especially for those seeking help in their darkest moments.
- **God's Protection is Ever-Present:** Through the visions I had, like the Black Horse and the lambs, God reminded me that staying close to Him offers protection. When we step away from His covering, we leave ourselves vulnerable.

Action Steps for You

Let's turn these lessons into action in your own life:

- **Examine Your Faith Journey:** Think about times when you've felt distant from God. What hurt or disappointment might be holding you back? Take those things to Him in prayer.

- **Heed God's Warnings in Your Life:** Pay attention to the ways God might be speaking to you—through dreams, signs, or a quiet nudge in your spirit. Ask Him for discernment to understand His guidance.
- **Be a Source of Compassion:** Look for opportunities to show empathy and kindness to others, especially those who are struggling. You might be the reflection of God's love they need to see.
- **Stay Close to God's Covering:** Are there areas in your life where you've distanced yourself from God? Take a step today to draw closer to Him, whether it's through prayer, repentance, or reconnecting with His Word.

Insights for Prayer

Here's how you can pray this week to grow in faith and understanding:

- **Pray for a Heart of Compassion:** Ask God to help you show His love and grace to those who are hurting or searching for Him.
- **Seek Forgiveness for Rejection:** If you've ignored God's guidance or walked away from Him, ask for forgiveness and strength to return to Him.
- **Ask for Spiritual Discernment:** Pray for the ability to hear God's voice clearly and to act on the guidance He gives.
- **Thank God for His Pursuit:** Spend time thanking Him for never giving up on you, even when you've wandered. His love and protection are always there, waiting for you to come back.

Chapter 4 Rejecting God and Christianity

Prompt: Reflect on how you can strengthen your relationship with God. Write one or more steps to deepen your faith or include a prayer seeking wisdom and trust in His plan.

_____
_____
_____
_____
_____
_____
_____
_____
_____
_____
_____
_____
_____
_____
_____
_____
_____
_____
_____
_____
_____
_____

Chapter 5

More Warnings from God

There were so many times in my life when God tried to warn me, but I ignored Him. He spoke to me in ways that should have been impossible to miss, yet I brushed them aside and continued in my ways. It wasn't until later that I realized how many of those warnings were meant to save me from trouble—or even to save my life.

One of those moments happened when I was on my way to get into one of those situation that would contribute to my downfall. I was in the car with my youngest son, DeAndre, driving toward a decision that could of landed me in serious trouble. As we were driving, I heard an audible voice tell me, "Turn around and go back."

It was so clear that I thought someone else had spoken. I asked DeAndre, "Did you say something?" and he said, "No, Dad, I didn't say anything."

The voice was so real that I actually pulled the car over, thinking someone might've been in the back seat. But when I checked, there was no one there. Even then, I didn't understand that it was God speaking to me, trying to steer me away from disaster. I ignored the warning and kept driving.

Looking back, I see that God was trying to protect me. He was giving me every opportunity to turn away from the path I was heading down, but I wasn't listening.

There was another time when God's protection was even more obvious, though I didn't recognize it at the moment. I got into it with a guy, and things escalated quickly. He left and came back with a shotgun. He stood about five feet away from me, aimed the gun, and pulled the trigger.

Nothing hit me.

At that distance, there was no way I should've walked away unharmed. Everyone around us was stunned. They couldn't believe what had just happened. My brother Reggie was there, and he came running over, asking, "Are you okay?" I just nodded and said, "Yeah, I'm good."

At the time, I shrugged it off, thinking I had just gotten lucky. But now, I know better. That wasn't luck—it was God protecting me. There was no other explanation for why I wasn't hurt in that situation.

Over and over again, God was there, guiding me and protecting me, even when I didn't realize it. Whether it was through a voice telling me to turn back, a dream warning me to stay on the right path, or physical protection in a life-threatening moment, He was always there.

I didn't always see it, though. I didn't recognize His hand in my life because I was too caught up in my own plans and my own struggles. I didn't understand that God was working for my good, even when I was ignoring Him.

Now, I see things differently. I can look back at those moments and recognize them for what they were—proof of God's love and protection. Even when I wasn't listening, He never stopped speaking. Even when I walked away, He never left me.

Anger at God

There was a time when I was angry—really angry—at God. It wasn't just frustration or disappointment; it was deep bitterness. I felt like He had let me down.

That bitterness started after I went to the church, desperate for help with my addiction and was told, "Your problem is simple—just stop sinning."I already knew I was sinning. That wasn't news to me. What I needed was someone to help me figure out how to stop and if God loved me, why would He let me be rejected like that?

I was also angry about the situations I found myself in. I looked at my life and thought, *If You love me, why am I going through all this?* I couldn't see that my own decisions had brought me to that point. All I saw was the pain, the struggle, and what felt like God's silence.

But now, looking back, I can see that God wasn't failing me—I was ignoring Him. He had been trying to guide me all along. He gave me warnings and opportunities to turn back, but I didn't listen. It wasn't God who abandoned me—it was me who walked away from Him.

There's a piece of writing I think about often now, the "Footprints in the Sand" poem. It's about a man who looks back over his life and sees two sets of footprints in the sand—his and God's. But during the hardest times, there's only one set of footprints. The man thinks God left him during those moments, but God tells him, "No, those were the times I carried you."

That's exactly how I feel now. I see all the times God carried me, even when I thought He wasn't there. I see how He was working in my life, orchestrating circumstances to protect me, to guide me, and to ultimately bring me back to Him.

It wasn't easy to admit that I had been wrong. It wasn't easy to take responsibility for my choices and recognize that God had been trying to help me all along. But once I did, everything changed. I stopped blaming God for my struggles and started trusting Him instead.

I understand now that God never stopped loving me. Even in my darkest moments, even when I was angry at Him, He was still there. He didn't give up on me, even when I gave up on myself.

Full Circle: Returning to God

What ultimately brought me back to God was the way the Holy Spirit revealed His presence, His love, and His protection to me. It wasn't a single moment—it was a series of revelations that showed me just how much He had been with me, even when I didn't realize it.

One of the first things God showed me was that He had been there all along. He opened my eyes to see how, even in my worst moments, He was working behind the scenes, protecting me and guiding me. He revealed His love in a way I had never understood before, and it overwhelmed me.

It wasn't just about me anymore, though. God began to show me that everything I had been through wasn't just for my benefit— it was also so I could help others. He had positioned me in such a way that my experiences, my pain, and my struggles could be used to bring hope and healing to other people.

I started to see God's hand in every part of my life. The pain I went through, the blessings I received, the people I met—it was all part of His plan. I realized that none of it was random. Every circumstance, every encounter, every trial was leading me closer to Him and preparing me for the purpose He had for my life.

Even meeting my wife was something I believe was orchestrated by God. When I look back on how we met and how everything came together, I see His fingerprints all over it. If even one thing had been different, we might never have crossed paths. But

God knew what He was doing. He knew the kind of woman I needed, someone who would stay by my side through everything, and He made sure we found each other.

Through it all, God showed me that He blesses us so that we can be a blessing to others. It's never just about us. Our lives, our experiences, our struggles—they're all meant to touch the lives of others. That's the kind of God we serve, a God who can take the broken pieces of our lives and turn them into something beautiful, something that brings hope and healing to the people around us.

I've learned that even in our darkest moments, if we turn to God, He will show Himself to be mighty and faithful. He'll bring us out of the pain, out of the struggle, and into a place where we can not only stand strong but also help others do the same.

Returning to God wasn't just about finding peace for myself. It was about stepping into the purpose He had for my life, a purpose that goes far beyond me. It's about showing others that no matter how far they've fallen, no matter how broken they feel, God is there, waiting to pick them up and lead them into something greater.

Chapter 5: Reflection Section: Lessons to Take Away

Here's what I want to share with you from this chapter—lessons that I've learned and that I hope will speak to your heart:

- **God Warns and Protects Even When We Ignore Him:** There were times when I didn't understand that God was speaking to me, like the voice I heard in the car or the shotgun incident. Looking back, I see how He warned and protected me, even when I wasn't paying attention.
- **Anger at God Often Stems from Misunderstanding:** I was bitter toward God because I didn't understand His silence or His plan. Over time, I realized He had been guiding and protecting me all along, even in ways I couldn't see at the time.
- **Ignoring God's Warnings Has Consequences:** When I chose to disregard God's guidance, it left me open to unnecessary pain and struggle. Obedience to Him isn't about restriction—it's about protection.
- **God's Love is Unwavering:** No matter how many times I rejected Him or got angry, God never abandoned me. His love carried me through my darkest moments.
- **Painful Experiences Can Have Purpose:** Everything I went through had a purpose. God used those trials to prepare me to offer hope and healing to others.

Action Steps for You

Take a moment to reflect and put these lessons into action in your own life:

- **Reflect on Past Warnings:** Think about times when you may have ignored God's guidance. How did those choices affect you? Consider how you can respond differently now.
- **Release Anger at God:** If you're holding onto bitterness or frustration toward God, take those feelings to Him in prayer. Ask Him to help you see the bigger picture.

- **Recognize God's Hand:** Look back at times when you were spared harm or when things unexpectedly worked out. See those moments as evidence of His love and protection.
- **Share Your Story:** Your experiences, both the hard times and the triumphs, can inspire and uplift others. Find someone who could benefit from hearing what you've been through.

Insights for Prayer

Here are some specific ways you can pray as you reflect on this chapter:

- **Pray for Sensitivity to God's Voice:** Ask God to make His guidance clear to you, and pray for the courage to follow it.
- **Seek Forgiveness for Ignoring God:** Bring moments of disobedience before Him and ask for a heart that listens and obeys.
- **Thank God for His Protection:** Spend time thanking Him for the ways He's shielded you, even when you didn't recognize it at the time.
- **Meditate on Jeremiah 29:11:** Let this scripture remind you that God's plans for you are always good, even when you're in the middle of difficult circumstances.

Chapter 5 More Warnings from God

Prompt: Think about the ways God might be speaking to you through circumstances or people. Write one or more goals to listen more closely and include a prayer for discernment.

Chapter 6

Forgiveness and Rebuilding My Family

The first year and a half I was incarcerated, my wife and I didn't communicate at all. During that time, she would bring the boys up to the jail where I was, but she wouldn't come in. When I was moved to Southampton Correctional Center, it was the same. She brought my kids and my mother to see me, and my mom would come in with the kids, but she wouldn't step inside.

That went on for about a year and a half to two years before we started talking again. During that time, I had it in my mind that my marriage was over. I thought, "I don't want anything to do with her." I even used to say, "I had a million women before I got here; I'll get a million more when I get out." That's where I was mentally. But God had a different plan.

Everywhere I turned, God was putting something about marriage in front of me. He was showing me the sanctity of marriage, the power and authority of it. One day, I came across a cassette program—a set of eight cassettes and a book called *Heirs Together* by Mac Hammond and Dr. Jack Hayford. They broke down marriage from a biblical perspective, starting with Genesis, where it says, "For this reason, a man shall leave his father and mother and cleave to his wife, and they shall become one flesh."

What struck me the most was something Dr. Hayford explained about the Hebrew language. Of the 233 root words in Hebrew, all but one are either masculine or feminine. The one word that encompasses both genders is Jehovah. He explained that man was created in the image of God, male and female, both components together. That's why God took Eve from Adam's rib—so they could come back together in a relationship that reflects the fullness of God. That revelation about God's design for marriage got to me.

As I learned more, I started praying for the restoration of my marriage. One day, my wife brought my mom and kids to visit me. As usual, she didn't come in. When I finished the visit and walked back out, I saw her pulling up just as I was leaving. She had gone to a store down the road and returned at the same time I was leaving. She later told me she didn't plan it that way—it just happened. When she saw me, she got out of the car and spoke to me.

She asked, "How are you doing?" and I asked her the same. After we exchanged a few words, I started to walk away, but then I turned back and asked if she was bringing the kids again next week. She said she was. I started to leave again, but something made me stop. I turned around and asked, "Are you coming in next time?" She hesitated but finally said, "Yeah, I'm coming in."

That moment was the beginning of God showing me what marriage could be. He was working on her heart, too, although I didn't know it then. She later told me that she'd been hearing from every direction that she needed to divorce me. But one woman, Patsy Winters, told her, "That's not what God wants for you." She said God didn't want her to get a divorce. Despite all the other voices telling her otherwise, she chose to listen to Patsy—and to God.

God showed me how powerful marriage is, the unity between a husband and wife, and the covenant it represents. From that point on, we started rebuilding our relationship. In fact, our marriage became stronger while I was in prison than it had ever been before, because we were both growing in Christ.

A Dream and Its Fulfillment

During this time, God gave me a dream. In the dream, my wife, my sons, and I were in the visitation room. It was just the four of us. I got up, hugged my boys, and turned to leave. As I was about to walk away, I looked back at my wife. She was standing there with her arms open. I walked back over to her, and we embraced.

At the time, we hadn't had any visits together, so it was just a dream. But not long after that, it came to pass. My wife came to visit me, and I was struggling with a lot of emotions. When she came in, I said to her, "I don't care what you do with your life. Move forward however you want. Just make sure I see my boys and that they stay in communication with me." I spent most of the visit talking to my boys, trying to make up for lost time.

At the end of the visit, I prayed for my boys and hugged them. As I turned around, I saw my wife standing there with her arms open. I walked over and hugged her. That was the exact moment God had shown me in my dream—the positions, the setting, even what she was wearing. Everything matched. It was the fulfillment of what He had promised me.

A Father's Apology

During that same visit, I took the opportunity to apologize to my sons. I knew the wrong I had done and the hurt I had caused them. I looked them in the eyes and said, "I've been wrong. I've done things that hurt you, and I wish I could take them back, but I can't. What I can do is ask for your forgiveness."

I also told them, "If you choose not to forgive me, I'll accept that. I won't like it, but I'll accept it. I just want you to know how sorry I am." My sons looked at me like I had two heads. Then they said, "Dad, we forgive you. We love you."

Hearing those words was one of the most gratifying moments of my life. It was also one of the hardest things I've ever had to do—admitting my failures and asking my children for forgiveness. But when they told me they loved me and forgave me, it felt like the weight of the world had been lifted off my shoulders.

A New Foundation

That visit marked the beginning of a new chapter in my life and in our family. It wasn't just about restoring my marriage—it was about rebuilding my entire family. God showed me the importance of humility, of being willing to admit my wrongs and seek forgiveness. He also showed me the power of His promises and how He can bring dreams to pass in ways we never expect.

My marriage and my relationship with my sons grew stronger from that point on. It wasn't easy, and it took time, but God's hand was in it every step of the way. He took what was broken and began to make it whole again, piece by piece.

Chapter 6: Reflection Section: Lessons to Take Away

Here's what I want you to reflect on from this chapter:

- **Forgiveness Unlocks Restoration:** Asking for forgiveness is a humbling process, but it's essential for rebuilding relationships. When I apologized to my sons, it opened the door for healing and a deeper connection with them.
- **God Can Rebuild What's Broken:** My marriage seemed irreparable, but God had other plans. Through His guidance and promises, we were able to create a stronger foundation than we'd ever had before.
- **Dreams Are Part of God's Promises:** The dream God gave me about reuniting with my wife wasn't just symbolic; it was His assurance of what was to come. Trusting in His vision brought hope and fulfillment.
- **Humility Leads to Healing:** Admitting my mistakes and seeking forgiveness was one of the hardest things I've ever done, but it was also one of the most freeing and transformative.
- **Marriage Reflects God's Unity:** Understanding the biblical significance of marriage helped me realize its sacredness and the role it plays in reflecting God's design and unity.

Action Steps for You

Take these steps to start rebuilding relationships and trusting God's promises:

- **Apologize Where Needed:** Think about someone you've hurt and take the first step toward mending that relationship. Acknowledge your wrongs and ask for forgiveness, even if it's difficult.

- **Pray for Restoration:** Bring your broken relationships to God. Ask Him to work in the hearts of everyone involved and to guide you in rebuilding trust and connection.
- **Hold on to God's Promises:** If God has given you a vision or dream for your future, write it down and trust that He will bring it to pass in His perfect timing.
- **Study the Biblical Meaning of Relationships:** Dive into scriptures about marriage, family, and unity. Let God's Word guide how you approach and nurture your relationships.
- **Walk in Humility:** Make a conscious effort to admit your mistakes and seek reconciliation, understanding that humility is key to healing and growth.

Insights for Prayer

- **Pray for Forgiveness and Healing:** Ask God to help you seek and extend forgiveness where it's needed, and pray for His hand in restoring broken relationships.
- **Seek Clarity in God's Promises:** Pray for understanding and patience as you wait for God to fulfill His promises in your life.
- **Ask for Unity in Relationships:** Lift up your marriage, family, or friendships, asking God to align them with His design and strengthen the bonds between you.
- **Thank God for His Faithfulness:** Reflect on how God has already worked in your life and relationships, and express gratitude for His guidance and grace.
- **Meditate on Genesis 2:24:** Let the truth of "becoming one flesh" inspire you to pursue unity and wholeness in your relationships as God intended.

God is always in the business of restoration, and no relationship is beyond His ability to heal and make whole. Trust Him, take the steps He's calling you to, and watch as He transforms your life and relationships.

Chapter 3 The Grip of Addiction

Prompt: Reflect on areas of your life where addiction—whether physical, emotional, or spiritual—may have taken hold. Write one or more goals for breaking free and include a prayer for strength and guidance.

Chapter 7

Spiritual Awakening

The Beginning of Spiritual Awakening

My spiritual awakening began while I was in jail. That's when it truly hit me—the turning point where I started to recognize God's hand in my life. It was in Suffolk Virginia jail during a time of intense soul-searching, that I experienced two distinct visitations from the Holy Spirit. He came into my jail cell twice, those moments revealed to me just how much God cared about me and loved me.

I began praying and asking God to show me the deeper reasons behind everything that had happened to me. "Lord, show me the spiritual consequences of my choices. Reveal what's happening in the spirit realm," I prayed. God started opening my eyes. He showed me how the enemy had been coming against me and my family for years. It wasn't just about the mistakes I'd made or the bad decisions

I'd taken—this was a spiritual battle, one that I had been completely unprepared for.

I remembered something from years earlier. In my ignorance, I had challenged Satan, telling him, "I can take you on." At the time, I didn't understand how foolish and dangerous that was. But now, my perspective had changed. I didn't back away from the fight, but I also realized that this battle wasn't one I could face alone. It was no longer about me taking Satan on—it was about Jesus and me together confronting him. That shift in understanding changed everything.

Renewing the Mind

Romans 12:2 became my anchor during this time: "Do not be conformed to this world, but be transformed by the renewing of your mind, so that you may prove what is the good, acceptable, and perfect will of God." My mind had been consumed by negativity and lies for years, but now I began to renew it through the Word of God. I realized that the way to fight back wasn't just through willpower but through transforming how I thought and saw the world.

I also became deeply aware of generational curses. I understood that the decisions I made would impact not only me but also my children, grandchildren, and even future generations. I became determined to stop the cycle. Whatever curses or strongholds had entered my life, I declared they would stop with me. They wouldn't touch my kids or anyone else in my bloodline. This determination became a cornerstone of my spiritual awakening.

Meeting Kelvin: A Spiritual Brother

When I was later transferred to Powhatan Correctional Center, I continued to grow. The first thing I did was look for a Bible study group, and I found one. That's also where I met Kelvin, who became one of the closest people to me outside of my family. But at first, I couldn't stand him. Something about his personality rubbed me the wrong way. When I was transferred to Southampton, I thought I was leaving him behind for good. But when I arrived, God told me to pray for Kelvin to join me there. I didn't want to, but I begrudgingly prayed, and sure enough, God brought him to Southampton.

When Kelvin arrived, our dynamics changed completely. We hit it off immediately, realizing that we were on similar spiritual journeys. We found out that the compound had a chapel, a building that felt more like a regular church than anything you'd expect to find in prison. Inside, there were pews, an altar, and even a library filled with books, audio recordings, and videos to help people grow spiritually.

Kelvin and I made a pact: nothing would interfere with our time in the chapel. We committed to going there every day to study, pray, and grow in our faith. However, there was a challenge. In prison, you're required to have a job or attend classes to maintain good time credits. Initially, I didn't know how we'd balance that requirement with our commitment to the chapel. But God was already working on our behalf.

One day, a staff member approached us about a job in the kitchen's laundry area. We hesitated because we didn't want it to take us away from the chapel. But when we met the kitchen supervisor, we discovered he was a Christian. We explained our priorities, and to our amazement, he told us we could go to the chapel anytime we needed. "Just let me know," he said. That kind of freedom in a prison environment was unheard of. It was a clear sign of God's favor.

Our time in the chapel became transformative. Every day, we immersed ourselves in the Word. We read books, listened to sermons, and watched videos that deepened our understanding of Scripture. I even began studying the Bible in a way I never had before. Using Greek and Hebrew concordances, I broke down passages word by word, writing out definitions and reading the verses with those definitions in mind. This practice opened up Scripture to me in a profound way. Over time, I became so familiar with the meanings that I no longer needed to look them up as often. The Word of God became alive to me.

One pivotal moment in my spiritual journey happened during a Sunday service. God told me to turn around and look at Kelvin. When I did, I saw him serving as an usher, humbly doing a task I had thought myself too good for. That realization hit me hard. After the service, I went back to my room, locked the door, and got down on my knees. I prayed, "God, whatever You want me to do, I'll do it. Just tell me what You want, and I'll obey."

Becoming a Leader in the Chapel

The very next week I was appointed as the coordinator for the Christian Discipleship Training Program, essentially becoming the leader of the Christian church on the compound. It wasn't a role I sought, but it became one of the most significant chapters of my life. Kelvin and I worked together as equals, building each other up and transforming the culture of the chapel.

God's favor extended beyond the Inmates. The staff trusted us in ways that were unusual in a prison setting. For example, there was a rule that no more than three people could gather in a room at a time. Yet, during our Bible studies, we'd have eight or nine people crammed into a room, and the officers would turn a blind eye. On one occasion, an officer locked the chapel doors and left us alone for a Bible study—something that simply didn't happen in prison. Another time, we prayed for a young officer who broke down in tears, saying, "I can't believe this. They trained us to be harsh with you, and here you are praying for me and my family." Moments like these showed how God was working through us to touch not only the inmates but also the staff.

Changing the Culture of the Chapel

Our time at Southampton was marked by growth, transformation, and leadership. Through studying Scripture and teaching others, we broke the power of agreement with lies and helped people see themselves as God saw them. We taught about renewing the mind, breaking generational curses, and stepping into the freedom God offers. Those years became the foundation for everything God had planned for me in the future.

Looking back, I can see how God used that season to refine me and prepare me for greater things. It wasn't just about my redemption—it was about helping others find their way to God. Prison became the place where I first truly experienced spiritual freedom, even while physically confined. It was a reminder that when we surrender to God, He can do far more than we ever imagined.

Chapter 7: Reflection Section: Lessons to Take Away

Let me share with you some key lessons I've learned from this chapter of my journey. I hope they resonate with you and encourage you in your walk:

- **Spiritual Awakening Begins in Surrender:** My transformation started when I opened my heart to God and sought His understanding. It was through surrender that I began to grow spiritually and gain revelation.
- **Renewing the Mind is Key to Freedom:** Romans 12:2 became my foundation. Changing my mindset and rejecting the enemy's lies allowed me to walk in freedom and align my thoughts with God's truth.
- **Generational Curses Can Be Broken:** I realized that my choices impacted more than just me—they affected future generations. Through prayer and faith, I stood in the gap to break cycles of addiction and brokenness in my bloodline.
- **God Places People in Our Lives for Growth:** My relationship with Kelvin was no coincidence. God used it to refine us both, proving that "iron sharpens iron" as we grew stronger together.
- **Favor Follows Obedience:** As Kelvin and I committed to prioritizing God, we experienced His favor in extraordinary ways. Obedience opened doors that changed not only us but the culture around us.

Action Steps for You

Here are some ways you can put these lessons into practice:

- **Seek God Daily:** Set aside time each day to connect with Him in prayer and through His Word. Ask Him to reveal the areas of your life that need transformation.
- **Renew Your Mind:** Challenge negative thoughts and replace them with God's truth. Meditate on Romans 12:2 and speak it over your life.

- **Declare Freedom for Your Family:** Pray to break generational cycles of sin or struggle. Declare that those patterns stop with you and that blessings flow to future generations.
- **Invest in Spiritual Relationships:** Surround yourself with people who will push you closer to God. Be open to the relationships He brings into your life for your growth.
- **Prioritize Obedience:** Follow God's leading, even when it's difficult or doesn't make sense. Trust that His favor will follow when you walk in His will.

Insights for Prayer

Here are some specific ways to guide your prayers:

- **Pray for a Renewed Mind:** Ask God to help you see yourself and your circumstances through His eyes, rejecting lies and embracing His truth.
- **Break Generational Cycles:** Bring any recurring struggles in your family to God, declaring freedom and blessing over your bloodline.
- **Thank God for His Favor:** Take time to thank Him for the ways He's already shown up in your life, even in the small things.
- **Seek God's Purpose in Relationships:** Pray for wisdom and discernment in building relationships that will strengthen your faith.
- **Meditate on Proverbs 27:17:** Let this verse remind you of the importance of relationships that challenge and encourage you to grow spiritually.

Chapter 7 Spiritual Awakening

Prompt: Identify one or more ways to grow spiritually. Write steps to foster renewal or include a prayer asking God to awaken your heart to His purpose.

Chapter 8

Spiritual Disciplines and Growth

Early Discipline and Study Practices

My spiritual growth really began to take shape during my first year at Southampton. It was there that I started developing the habits and disciplines that would help me grow closer to God. Every morning, I had a routine: I'd grab my Bible, my concordances, and any other resources I had, and I'd head to a table in the hallway. There, I'd spend hours studying the Word of God.

I would take a scripture and break it down completely. I'd write out the verses, leaving space between each word, and then I'd go through and write down the definitions of each word. This helped me understand the deeper meanings in the scriptures and gave me a clearer picture of what God was saying through His Word.

One thing I remember vividly about my time there was how much I actually looked forward to lockdowns. Lockdowns happened during major shakedowns, usually once a quarter, when we'd be confined to our cells for three days straight. Most people hated those times, but for me, they were opportunities to focus entirely on God. During lockdowns, I would fast, pray, and spend hours in my Bible. I used those times to seek God's guidance, to ask for wisdom, and to understand His Word on a deeper level.

In addition to my personal study, I joined group Bible studies and taught the

corporate Bible studies at the Chapel. Those times of fellowship and learning were essential in keeping me spiritually grounded. Being able to share insights, ask questions, and hear others' perspectives helped me grow even more.

As I developed these daily practices, my hunger for God's Word only grew stronger. It was like the more I learned, the more I realized how much there was still to learn. I became determined to stay consistent in these disciplines because I could see the difference they were making in my life.

These early routines were the foundation for everything that followed. They helped me build a relationship with God that wasn't based on emotion or circumstance, but on His Word and His promises. It was in these moments of quiet study and prayer that I began to truly understand who God is and who He created me to be.

Seeking Truth Through Discipline

By my second or third year at Southampton, my spiritual journey had intensified. I had developed a deep hunger for the truth of God's Word, and I was willing to do whatever it took to learn. That hunger drove me to seek out teachings and spiritual insights, even in the most unlikely ways.

One discovery changed everything for us. The prison didn't have cable, but we found that certain nights, under specific conditions, the TBN (Trinity Broadcasting Network) signal would bleed through. If the weather was clear, we could sometimes tune in and catch the broadcast. Whenever that happened, we would let each other know so no one missed it.

I remember one night in particular. Around 9:30 p.m., someone came and told me that TBN was on. I immediately turned it on and saw a preacher teaching about the blessings of Abraham. I was captivated. The teaching was deep, and it spoke directly to my spirit. I stayed up all night waiting for the broadcast to come back on, knowing from experience that it would be repeated in the early morning hours. Sure enough, around 6:00 a.m., it aired again.

The preacher walked through Galatians 3, explaining how, through Christ, the blessings of Abraham now belong to us. Then he connected it to Genesis 14, where Melchizedek blessed Abraham. He broke down the blessings of dominion, elevation, and inheritance. I learned how God gave Abraham victory over his enemies, made him a father of many nations, and empowered him with grace—symbolized by the addition of the fifth letter, representing grace, to his name.

This was the kind of dedication we had to seek the truth. We were willing to stay up all night, hoping for a faint signal from a cable station just to receive a word from God. That's how serious we were about growing spiritually.

Receiving Support from Family

Even though I was in prison, my spiritual growth was never a solo journey. My family played an important role in supporting me, even from the outside. They were a big part of why I could continue to grow spiritually, despite the limitations of my environment.

The Chapel library at Southampton was a gift from God. It had almost everything we needed to study the Word—books, audio teachings, and other resources. But there were some things it didn't have, and that's where my family stepped in. My wife and my sisters, Doris and Carolyn, made sure I had what I needed.

I remember one instance when I wanted a specific book but couldn't receive it in the usual way. The prison had strict rules about mail: letters couldn't exceed five pages. But my sisters figured out a workaround. They printed the book out in sections and mailed me five pages at a time until I had the entire thing. That's the kind of commitment they had to my growth.

Their support wasn't just about sending books—it was about standing with me in faith. Every time they sent something, I knew it was another way they were saying, "We believe in you, and we believe in what God is doing in your life."

Even in prison, God made sure I had everything I needed to grow closer to Him. Whether it was through the Chapel resources or my family's love and effort, He provided. Looking back, I see how God used those moments to show me that He never abandons us.

The Christian Coalition and Challenging the Odds

At Southampton, I found myself surrounded by a group of men who became my closest allies in faith. These were men with serious sentences—some with hundreds of years, life without parole, or no hope of release according to the state. But together, we formed a bond rooted in the Word of God.

People on the outside of the group called us "The Christian Coalition," while others in the prison sometimes mocked us, calling us the "Bible Boys" or "Randy's Knights." It didn't matter to us what they called us because we were focused on growing spiritually and challenging the impossible.

One of the first things I told the group was not to accept their circumstances as final. I didn't care if they had life sentences or no parole; we were going to stand on the promises of God and believe for a breakthrough. Even the men who technically had no way out began praying and declaring that their situations would change.

There were about ten of us in the group, and one by one, I started to see God move. The man with a life sentence? He's home now. Another man with 600 years? He's home too. At first, it felt impossible, but we kept studying the Word, praying, and encouraging each other.

We studied scriptures that reminded us of God's power to turn the hearts of leaders. Proverbs 21:1 became a cornerstone for us: "The king's heart is in the hand of the Lord; He directs it like a watercourse wherever He pleases." We prayed that God would touch the hearts of those in positions of authority—the judges, parole boards, and government officials—and change their minds.

One of the most remarkable stories came from our prayers for a Virginia Beach prosecutor. This man had been known for his harsh stance, famously saying, "Lock them up and throw away the key." He had no interest in second chances or rehabilitation.

But as we prayed, we started to see a shift. That same man eventually became a state senator and a vocal advocate for second chances. He went from being one of the most rigid voices in the justice system to someone who actively worked to help people get out of prison and rebuild their lives.

The power of prayer and our unwavering belief in God's promises became evident in so many ways. Watching those around me go home, even the ones who were told they'd never leave prison, showed me that with God, nothing is impossible.

Appointed to Serve: Becoming an Inmate Advisor

One day, while I was working in the prison kitchen, I heard about a position opening up for an inmate advisor. In prison, an inmate advisor acts as a kind of advocate, helping other prisoners navigate the disciplinary process.

Curious, I asked what the job entailed. The officer told me there wasn't an opening after all, so I didn't think much of it. But the following week, I received institutional mail saying I had been reassigned to the position of inmate advisor. At first, I was angry. "They didn't even ask me!" I thought.

When I confronted the hearing officer about it, he said, "I looked at your record and talked to people about you. You're perfect for this job." I didn't see it at the time, but this was God opening another door.

The job allowed me to interact with inmates who wouldn't normally come to church or Bible study. Many of them were in trouble or facing punishment, and this gave me the chance to speak life into their situations.

The Hearings officer also told me, "I know how much you like going to the Chapel. Don't worry—you can still go whenever you want. Just let us know, and we'll make it work." This was another example of God's favor.

This position wasn't just a job—it became a ministry. I was able to help other inmates, encourage them, and point them toward God, even in the middle of their struggles.

God's Favor in Action

Throughout my time at Southampton, God's favor was evident in ways I couldn't ignore. Whether it was being reassigned to a position that allowed me to minister to others or witnessing the transformation of those around me, I could see His hand at work.

One of the most significant examples was seeing men with no chance of parole find freedom. Watching the prosecutor who once said, "Lock them up and throw away the key," become an advocate for second chances showed me the power of prayer and faith.

Even in the smallest moments—like finding books on marriage exactly when I needed them or being able to study uninterrupted in the Chapel—I saw God's love and guidance.

Every step of the way, He was teaching me that His plans are bigger than anything I could imagine. And through the spiritual disciplines I developed, I was learning to trust Him completely.

Chapter 8: Reflection Section: Lessons to Take Away

Let me share some important lessons from this chapter of my journey that I believe can inspire and encourage you:

- **Spiritual Growth Requires Discipline:** My daily practices of studying Scripture, praying, and fasting showed me that true spiritual growth comes from consistent effort. It's in those quiet, dedicated moments that transformation happens.
- **God's Favor Opens Doors:** I saw firsthand how God's favor made a way for me, whether it was access to the Chapel or being placed in roles where I could serve others. His hand opened opportunities I couldn't have imagined.
- **Support from Loved Ones Matters:** My family's faith and commitment—sending me books and standing with me in prayer—proved that having a strong support system makes all the difference in personal and spiritual growth.
- **Marriage Restoration is Possible with God:** Even in prison, God worked miracles in my marriage. No relationship is too broken for Him to heal when you place it in His hands.
- **Prayer Can Change the Impossible:** I witnessed the power of prayer transform hardened hearts, open doors for parole, and change lives. Persistent, faith-filled prayer makes the impossible possible.

Action Steps for You

Here are some practical ways you can apply these lessons to your own life:

- **Develop Consistent Spiritual Practices:** Carve out time each day to connect with God through prayer, Scripture, and reflection. Even a few minutes of focused time with Him can make a big difference.
- **Stand in Faith for Restoration:** Whatever feels broken—whether a relationship, your health, or another area of life—bring it to God and trust Him to restore it. Pray specifically and trust His timing.

- **Surround Yourself with Support:** Lean on people who encourage your faith and hold you accountable. A strong support system can be a lifeline during tough times.
- **Speak Life Over Difficult Situations:** Declare God's promises over the things in your life that feel impossible. Trust that He is working, even when you can't see it.
- **Look for Opportunities to Serve:** Whether in a formal role or through small acts of kindness, find ways to serve and encourage others.

Insights for Prayer

Here are some ways to guide your prayers and strengthen your connection with God:

- **Pray for Spiritual Growth:** Ask God to help you establish routines and disciplines that bring you closer to Him and to reveal His truths as you study His Word.
- **Pray for Restoration:** Bring any broken relationships or challenging situations to God, asking Him for healing, guidance, and reconciliation.
- **Thank God for His Favor:** Take a moment to reflect on the ways God has already worked in your life and express your gratitude for His blessings.
- **Pray for Bold Faith:** Ask God to grow your faith so you can confidently speak His promises over your life and trust Him to handle the outcome.
- **Meditate on Proverbs 21:1:** This verse reminds us that God can move the hearts of even those in authority, aligning circumstances with His will for your life. Trust in His power to orchestrate what seems impossible.

Chapter 8 Spiritual Disciplines and Growth

Prompt: Write about one or more spiritual disciplines to focus on. Include a prayer asking for commitment and consistency in these practices.

_____
_____
_____
_____
_____
_____
_____
_____
_____
_____
_____
_____
_____
_____
_____
_____
_____
_____
_____
_____
_____
_____

Chapter 9

God's Power Behind Bars

By the time this part of my story unfolded, I had been incarcerated for about three, maybe three and a half years. That's when I began to see how God was elevating me within the body of Christ—even in this prison environment. I wasn't seeking out these roles, but time after time, circumstances showed me that God was moving through me to influence both inmates and staff.

Divine Appointments in Ministry

I was placed in positions that I never asked for. I became the coordinator for the Christian discipleship program—a role that brought me in contact with men who might never have set foot in a church, and I also became an inmate advisor. In both of these roles, I saw that God had planned this out. It wasn't about me at all. It was clear that He wanted to use me to spread His word and show His grace even in a place where hope seemed scarce.

I remember my first day in the discipleship program. Walking into that small chapel, I felt an undeniable pull as if I was stepping directly into God's plan. Later, as an inmate advisor, I sat down with guys who rarely cared about religion. They were angry, bitter, and often lost. Yet, in our talks—even during times of disciplinary hearings—I saw God working. He opened doors where there seemed to be none, and every conversation became a little more hopeful.

A Confrontation That Changed Perspectives

One incident stands out. Two inmates were locked up for cussing at Major Thorne—the same major known for his own frequent outbursts. I couldn't understand it. If Major Thorne

cussed every day, how could these guys be punished for doing what he did?

Driven by a conviction to set things straight, I approached the hearing officer and asked if I could speak to the major. I walked past the other staff offices, knocked on the door, and once inside, I told him, "Major, I have a problem. You locked up these two guys for cussing at you, but I know you probably cussed at them first." He looked at me, laughed a bit, and replied, "Man, go back and talk to Billy Seal," the hearing officer. Soon after, the major came by the hearing office and said I'm too tired to deal with this. Tear up the charges if you want, and let them go."

That moment wasn't about my ego; it was a lesson that God's favor can break through even in unexpected ways. It showed me that when you step in to stand for what's right, even those in authority can be touched by a different kind of power—a power that comes not from intimidation, but from truth.

Unexpected Encounters During Lockdown

Prison rules are strict, especially during lockdown. One evening, while I was being escorted between buildings, an officer stopped and called me "King of Southampton." I was taken aback. "Don't call me that! I'm no king of this place," I snapped.

Later that night, I reflected on the exchange. The Holy Spirit made it clear that the officer wasn't mocking me but was acknowledging something deeper—an unseen favor at work. I went back to see him and apologized for my reaction, and he explained that he saw something in me that He could not explain. That moment, small as it may have seemed, confirmed that God's favor was not hidden; even in jokes or casual remarks, it appeared unexpectedly.

Mentoring Those in Need

My role as an inmate advisor was not without its challenges, but it was here I saw God work miracles. Many of the men I mentored were angry, in trouble, or outright rejected any notion of religion. Yet, day by day, I witnessed transformation. I remember a young man with a history of anger and multiple infractions. The hearing officer was set to impose a severe punishment, but he offered this young man a 90-day chance under my guidance instead.

At first, the young man resisted everything I tried to do. He didn't trust me, and he didn't trust what I had to offer. But over time, as I consistently sat with him and shared lessons from the Bible, something changed. He began coming to church, asking questions, and when the 90 days were over, he didn't walk away. Instead, he stayed on—an example of how even the hardest hearts can be softened by genuine care and a little bit of divine grace.

I've also seen this work with those in positions we wouldn't normally expect. One night, a young correctional officer, overwhelmed by personal and financial pressures, came to me in confidence. He admitted that he was considering actions he knew could ruin his life, feeling desperate to bridge a gap between what he had and what he needed. For hours, we talked through his problems. I asked him if He wanted to trade the uniform He was wearing for the one I had on, jokingly. I also asked him if he was willing to give up everything he stood for. That conversation made a difference, and about a month later, he left corrections. I'm not exactly sure what his future holds, but I like to believe that night marked a turning point—a quiet victory for God's intervention.

More Than a Series of Incidents

As my time passed, these events began to stitch together a larger picture. I wasn't just an inmate with a bit of faith; I was becoming a part of something bigger. One day, about 7 years into my sentence after being transferred to Deerfield correction center I was told to go see Major Mays we had only talked in passing. I do not know what to expect.

When I arrived, the major greeted me by closing the door behind us and inviting me into his office. He pulled out a Bible from his desk and said, "The Holy Spirit told me to help you." That wasn't a scripted conversation; it was real, raw, and it shook me. Here was a man who wielded authority, taking a step to share his belief and offer his help because he felt moved by God. It wasn't just about following orders; it was about recognizing that each of us has a part in a bigger plan—even here, in prison.

That moment, along with others like the "King of Southampton" comment, wasn't repeated to boast or dramatize my experience. Instead, these were everyday reminders that God's favor, though subtle sometimes, was always present. And every time I encountered one of these moments, I was reminded to keep my focus on what really mattered—being faithful to the calling He'd placed on my life.

The Cost of Compassion and the Weight of Decisions

Not every interaction ended in immediate change or clear victory. There were darker times too, moments when trying to do the right thing came with heavy costs. I remember a Tuesday night Bible study where one inmate, clearly troubled, shared his ordeal. He told me how he'd been transferred among several institutions, always feeling watched, suspecting that someone was trying to poison him.

His voice was low and desperate as he admitted that he planned to kill the person he believed was spying on him.

I struggled with what to do next. Part of me wanted to warn the staff immediately, but I also knew that doing so might isolate him further. I spent days praying and wrestling with the decision until one night, a code 10-33 was called over the loudspeakers. In the chaos that followed, I later learned that the man had carried out his plan—he stabbed the person he suspected. Thankfully, the victim survived, but the consequences were severe.

At his hearing, the inmate requested me as his advisor. I met with him beforehand and told him, "There's nothing I can do to change this outcome—just stay quiet and let things run their course." I did my best to represent him, but deep inside, I wondered if an earlier decision might have prevented the tragedy. That experience taught me that even with God's favor, sometimes the results aren't what we hoped for, and that every choice carries a weight that we must bear.

Interweaving Experiences: A Cohesive Journey

Over time, the various experiences in prison—whether it was confronting authority, mentoring those in need, or facing the consequences of decisions made under pressure—began to form a continuous narrative. It wasn't about single, isolated events, but about a pattern: every moment was a chance for God to work, even when it wasn't immediately obvious.

I began to see that the repeated references to God's favor were not redundant. Each event, whether it was the minor comment of an officer or a major meeting with someone like Major Mays, added layers to my understanding of God's presence. What initially felt like the same message over and over was, in fact, a gradual unfolding of a much larger truth: that God's power moves in ways that sometimes need to be seen from different angles to be fully understood.

For instance, after the incident with the cussing charges, I spent hours thinking about the nature of authority and accountability. Later, in quiet moments during lockdown, when an officer's offhand remark echoed in my mind, I recognized that these were not just isolated incidents but parts of a whole narrative. They told the story of how authority could be questioned and rebuilt on the foundation of divine truth.

A Lasting Impact on Lives and Systems

Even as I continued my work, I observed changes beyond my immediate control. Inmates who had once been hardened by years of just trying to survive began to soften their stances. A few even started coming forward for Bible studies and discussions, intrigued by the transformation they witnessed in their peers. The small victories accumulated, each one a sign of a larger change sparked by God's work.

On the staff side, the effects were equally noticeable. Major Thorne wasn't the only one whose approach shifted. Over time, other officers began to show small gestures of respect—a nod here, a brief conversation there—that hinted at a deeper understanding of the possibility of redemption. These changes, subtle as they were, reinforced for me that God's work wasn't confined to the inmates alone. It touched everyone inside these walls, reshaping hearts in ways we couldn't predict.

I kept records of many of these encounters, not as a way to boast, but as a testimony to the tangible impact of faith in an environment defined by its harshness. Those notes reminded me that every soul, whether on the inside or among the guards, carried burdens that sometimes only God's grace could ease. They served as evidence that even in a place built to break men, there remained the power to build them up again.

In Conclusion

This chapter of my life is not about me; it's about what God accomplished through me in a place that few would expect to see grace. It's a reminder that no matter how confined we may appear, the spirit is free—and when we yield to that calling, even the most unlikely places can become grounds for transformation and hope.

May anyone reading this come to understand that change is possible, that every person—whether an inmate or a guard—carries the potential to be touched by God's hand. And as I continue on my journey, I hold fast to the belief that even behind bars, the light of God's love shines bright, breaking down walls and building up lives in ways we never imagined.

Chapter 9: Reflection Section: Lessons to Take Away

Let me share some key lessons from this chapter of my journey that I hope will inspire you to see how God can work in your life too:

- **God's Favor Transcends Circumstances:** Even in the most unlikely places, like prison, I experienced God's favor through unexpected roles, relationships, and opportunities. This shows that God's power knows no limits.
- **Every Moment is a Ministry Opportunity:** Whether I was mentoring an inmate or helping an officer in need, I realized that every interaction could be an opportunity to share God's love and wisdom.
- **Transformation is Possible for All:** I saw God's grace change the hearts of both inmates and staff. No one is beyond the reach of His love and healing.
- **Courage to Stand for What's Right:** Addressing injustices, even with authority figures, was challenging but necessary. It reminded me that standing for truth allows God to work through us.
- **Small Acts Lead to Big Impacts:** It was often the quiet moments—mentoring, listening, or simply showing up—that carried the greatest weight in transforming lives and fostering hope.

Action Steps for You

Here are some steps you can take to apply these lessons in your own life:

- **Trust God's Timing and Placement:** Even if your current situation feels limiting, trust that God has a purpose for you being there. Look for ways to serve and grow right where you are.
- **Stand for Truth:** When you see something wrong, don't shy away. Ask God for wisdom and courage to address injustices with grace and confidence.

- **Be a Mentor or Encourager:** Think of someone in your life who might need guidance or support, and make a commitment to walk with them through their journey.
- **Stay Attuned to Divine Appointments:** Pay attention to the small, everyday moments—they might be God's way of using you to make an impact.
- **Celebrate Transformation:** Whether you see changes in yourself or those around you, take time to thank God and acknowledge the work He's doing.

Insights for Prayer

Here are some specific ways you can pray to align with God's will and see His work in your life:

- **Pray for Discernment:** Ask God to help you recognize the opportunities He gives you to serve and share His love.
- **Pray for Courage:** Seek His strength to boldly stand for truth and righteousness, even in difficult situations.
- **Pray for the Hardened Heart:** Lift up those who seem resistant to change, asking God to soften their hearts and open their eyes to His love.
- **Thank God for His Favor:** Take time to reflect on where you've seen His hand at work in your life, and express gratitude for His guidance and provision.
- **Meditate on 2 Corinthians 12:9:** Let this verse remind you that God's power is made perfect in your weakness, giving you the strength to face any challenge.

Chapter 9 God's Power Behind Bars

Prompt: Reflect on challenges you're facing and write one or more ways to rely on God's strength to overcome them. Add a prayer seeking His guidance and power.

Chapter 10

When Rules Bend for Grace

A Special Visit in the Midst of Loss

It was a Tuesday, right before the 4:00 count, when an officer approached me. He told me I had two family members waiting to see me. Immediately, I knew something was wrong. I asked, "Is everything okay?" The officer didn't answer me. I asked him again, "Is it my mom?" He nodded his head, confirming what I feared.

After the count cleared, I was taken down to the treatment area, to the watch commander's office, where Annette and my sister Evelyn were waiting. As soon as I walked in, I could see it in their faces. They told me the news. My mom had passed away.

What stood out about this moment wasn't just the weight of the loss but the visit . Visits like this , especially after 4:00, were not allowed under normal circumstances. But the staff made an exception. Annette later told me, the Warden said "If it had been anybody else, they wouldn't have let them in. But because it was you, they allowed it."

That moment wasn't just about grief; it was a testament to God's favor. The way the staff bent the rules for my family showed me that God's hand was on me, even in the darkest moments. It reminded me that He was always working behind the scenes, orchestrating what seemed impossible.

Breaking the Rules for the Right Reasons

Prison life operates on a set of unwritten rules, the biggest one being: *mind your business.* If you intervene in someone else's affairs, you risk making enemies or worse. But when I saw someone in need, I couldn't just stand by.

One day, a young white inmate came in, and I noticed he was gravitating toward two predators. These men had a reputation, and I knew exactly what they were up to. I pulled the young boy aside and said, *You need to stay away from them. They're not your friends.*

He didn't believe me. *They wouldn't do that to me,* he said.

I wasn't about to let it go. I walked him over to the men and confronted them directly. *I know what you're trying to do,* I said. *Leave him alone.*

The boy finally understood after that encounter and kept his distance.

Intervening in situations like that wasn't easy. It went against the so-called "rules" of prison life. But I knew I had to follow God's rules, not man's. Time and time again, God gave me the courage and the wisdom to stand up for what was right, even when it put me at risk.

Mentorship and Transformation

One of the most rewarding aspects of my time in prison was witnessing lives transformed by God's grace.

There was a man deeply entrenched in the "game"—prison slang for engaging in homosexual activities. I approached him and said, *This isn't the life God has for you. You're better than this, and you can change.*

At first, he resisted. He didn't want to hear it, and I could tell he was defensive. But over time, something shifted. He started attending church, left that lifestyle behind, and recommitted his life to God.

Another time, a young white inmate came to Bible study, visibly upset. When I asked him what was wrong, he told me someone had stolen his belongings. He felt defeated, like he couldn't catch a break.

Don't worry. We'll get your things back, I assured him. I worked with some other inmates, and we made sure his belongings were returned.

I told him, *God hasn't forgotten about you. You're here for a reason.*

Moments like these reminded me why God placed me there. Prison wasn't just a place of punishment; it was a mission field.

Watching people grow and change through God's grace showed me that even in the darkest places, light can shine.

Every conversation, every act of kindness, and every moment of mentorship became a testament to God's power to transform lives.

Favor with Authority

Even the prison staff treated me differently because of God's favor. One officer in particular, Officer Jacobs, stood out. He had a reputation for provoking inmates, pushing them until they lashed out, just so he could write them up. I confronted him directly one day.

You can't keep doing this to people, I told him. *You're supposed to maintain order, not create chaos.*

Surprisingly, he listened. From that point on, he changed his approach. Not only did he stop antagonizing inmates, but he started consulting me before issuing charges. Another example of the favor of God was the hearing officer calling me over to His office giving me a bunch of charges inmates had caught their records and sending me to the buildings to talk with them about their charges and giving me the power to offer them a plea or dismiss them

He trusted me to go around, speak to the inmates, and make fair decisions. On one occasion, after reviewing a case, I told him, *This guy isn't guilty. You should dismiss this charge.* He agreed, respecting my judgment.

This level of trust and responsibility was unheard of in prison. It wasn't just about the power; it was about the opportunity to make a difference. God had placed me in a position where I could act as a mediator, ensuring fairness and justice in an environment where both were rare. It showed how God can work through anyone, even in the most unexpected places, to bring about change.

A Father's Connection

One of the most powerful examples of God's favor was the connection I maintained with my children despite being behind bars.

I told my son Randy, *If you ever need me, call here* . tell the officer to tell me to call home, one day He did just that. He was going through a rough time, dealing with a girl who He was having a rough time deciding whether to walk away from or stay with.

Dad, I need to see you. I can't do this over the phone, he said.

I went to the hearing office and spoke to Ms. Watson. I explained the situation, and she promised to talk to the assistant warden, Mr. Brown. She called me back later and said, *Tell Randy to be here at 1:00. He can visit you.*

Within hours, Randy was sitting across from me, pouring his heart out. He stayed until just before the 4:00 count, and we talked about everything he was going through. That kind of privilege was unheard of in prison, but God made it happen.

Other inmates couldn't believe it. They asked, *How did you get your son up here on a Monday?* I just smiled, knowing it was God's favor. Moments like that reminded me that God was always working behind the scenes, making ways for me to be the father my children needed, even from behind bars.

117

Grace in Action

Throughout my time in prison, God's grace was evident in so many ways. Whether it was through mentorship, protection, or favor with staff, He used me to make a difference in a place many consider hopeless.

From helping inmates find their way back to God, to protecting vulnerable individuals, to being trusted by officers to mediate disputes, every moment reflected God's hand at work.

These experiences taught me that even in the darkest places, God's light can shine. His grace doesn't just change lives; it transforms hearts, restores dignity, and proves that no situation is beyond His reach.

Chapter 10: Reflection Section: Lessons to Take Away

Let me share with you the key lessons God has revealed to me during my journey, and I pray they will resonate in your heart as well:

- **God's Favor Breaks Rules:** I've seen God's grace in action, bending man-made rules to show His love—whether it was allowing me a special visit after my mother's passing or providing a way to comfort my son during his tough times. His favor knows no bounds.
- **Standing Up for Others Reflects God's Heart:** By intervening to protect vulnerable inmates or confronting injustices, I've witnessed how God honors our willingness to stand for righteousness, even when it comes at personal risk.
- **Transformation Through Mentorship:** Watching lives change as I mentored others showed me how God can use us as vessels of His grace to reach and redeem even those who seem the most lost.
- **God's Light Shines in the Darkest Places:** No matter the challenges or confines of our surroundings, God's grace has proven to be a beacon of hope, bringing restoration and purpose to the most unlikely places.

Action Steps for You

Here are some ways you can apply these lessons in your own life:

- **Step Into Someone's Struggle:** Is there someone in your life who needs protection, guidance, or encouragement? Pray for the courage to stand up for them and trust God to guide your actions.
- **Be Open to Mentorship:** Whether you're guiding someone or being guided yourself, seek relationships that draw you closer to God. Share your faith and allow Him to use you as a light in someone else's journey.

- **Reflect God's Grace in Action:** Look for opportunities to demonstrate God's love through kindness, advocacy, or simple acts of protection. Even small gestures can have a profound impact.
- **Recognize God's Favor:** Reflect on how God has opened doors for you in tough times. Let those moments inspire gratitude and a renewed desire to share His goodness with others.

Insights for Prayer

Use these prayer points to connect with God and seek His direction:

- **Pray for Boldness:** Ask God to give you the courage to stand for righteousness, even when it's risky or challenging.
- **Seek Wisdom in Mentorship:** Pray for discernment and the right words as you guide or encourage others, trusting God to work through you.
- **Thank God for His Favor:** Reflect on the moments when His grace has shown up powerfully in your life. Thank Him for His blessings and trust Him to continue providing.
- **Ask for God's Presence in Dark Places:** Pray for His light to shine in areas of darkness, whether in your life, your community, or the lives of others, and trust Him to bring transformation and hope.

Chapter 10 When Rules Bend for Grace

Prompt: Reflect on a time when God's grace made the impossible possible. Write one or more goals to trust Him more deeply and include a prayer of gratitude.

_____
_____
_____
_____
_____
_____
_____
_____
_____
_____
_____
_____
_____
_____
_____
_____
_____
_____
_____
_____
_____

Chapter 11

How Are You Going to Stop God's Will?

One of the things I've learned in my walk with God is this: if you accept His will and walk in it, it can't be stopped. I firmly believe there are only two beings in the universe who can stop the will of God one is God Himself, and He won't, and us, through our choices. Beyond that, no power, no person, and no force can stand in the way of what God is doing.

In prison, I experienced this truth over and over. God's will was clear in my life. It was His will for me to have favor, to be safe, and to be respected—even in an environment where respect wasn't often given. One particular situation demonstrated this truth in ways I'll never forget.

Standing Up for Integrity

It all started one day during count time. I was in the bathroom area with another inmate. If you happened to be in the bathroom during count, the officers would count you there. That day, the officer on duty came in, counted us, and left, but as he walked away, I heard him say, "Something funny is going on in there."

The statement wasn't just casual; it was said loud enough for others to hear. Another inmate immediately commented, "Oh, you messed up now. Randy heard that, and he's not gonna let it go."

When the count cleared, I approached the officer and told him directly, "I heard what you said, and I didn't like it. I want you to apologize, and I want you to do it in front of everybody, because you said it in front of everybody."

The officer refused, and I knew I couldn't let it slide. It wasn't about ego—it was about integrity. I filed a formal complaint against him for defaming my character. In prison, you can write up staff just like they can write you up. My complaint stated that his comments were an attack on my reputation, particularly because I was in a leadership role and mentoring other inmates. I saw it as an attempt by the enemy to discredit me and undermine the work I was doing.

Seeking Justice Through the System

The complaint went to Sergeant Blanks, who was responsible for trying to resolve these kinds of issues. He called me into his office and asked me what had happened. I explained the situation, just as I've explained it here. Blanks then called the officer to get his side of the story. Over the phone, the officer admitted to making the comment but claimed he was joking.

Blanks told me, "He said he didn't mean anything by it, but he's willing to apologize." I replied, "I don't want just a private apology. I want him to apologize in front of everyone, just like he made the comment in front of everyone."

Later, we went to the treatment area where the officer was supposed to apologize. Instead, he changed his story. He denied saying anything inappropriate, claiming the complaint was unfounded. I told the sergeant, "Fine. I'll appeal it to the next level. I'm not letting this go."

Favor in High Places

As I waited for the appeal process to move forward, something remarkable happened. Major Mays—the same man who had told me earlier in my incarceration that the Holy Spirit had instructed him to help me—called me over one day.

He told me, "If any of my officers cross you or say anything disrespectful, you come directly to me." At the time, I didn't know if he'd seen my complaint or if this was unrelated, but his words reassured me that God's favor was still at work.

Shortly after, Captain Graves—one of the highest-ranking officers on the compound—called me to the watch commander's office. Holding my complaint in his hand, he said, "White, I know you. If you wrote this, you did it for a purpose. What do you want us to do about it? Do you want us to give him three or four days off with no pay? What do you want?"

I told him, "I don't want him punished. I just want him to apologize. If he apologizes to me, I'll let it go."

Graves nodded and said, "Alright, I'll make it happen."

A Public Apology and God's Glory

Not long after that, the officer came to me while I was in the housing area. He started to apologize privately, but I stopped him. "No," I said, "you made your comment in front of everybody, so you're going to apologize in front of everybody."

He walked over to where a group of inmates was gathered and, reluctantly, gave his apology. "I was just joking," he said, "there was nothing funny going on in the bathroom."

As he turned to leave, he stopped, looked back at me, and said, "I've never seen an inmate with this much power."

I replied, "You've never seen an inmate with this much faith in God."

That moment wasn't just about an apology. It was about showing how God's will works, even in a place like prison. It was a testament to how standing firm in faith and integrity can lead to outcomes that human authority can't explain.

Boldness Through Faith

One of the things God gives when you truly walk in His will is boldness. In prison, boldness isn't always welcomed. People expect you to follow certain unspoken rules, but I wasn't living by those rules. I was living by God's word.

There were a lot of different religious groups at the correction centers and They often held unity meetings where different religious groups—Christians, Muslims, Rastafarians, and others—would come together to discuss common issues. I never attended these meetings because, in my view, there is no true unity without Christ.

One day, the leader of the Muslims called me over and asked, "What do you think of the Prophet Mohammed?"

I looked him straight in the eye and said, "Do you really want to know?"

He said, "Yeah, I do."

I replied, "I think absolutely nothing of him. I think he was a grown man married to a 10-year-old child. You tell me what you think about that."

By this point, a group of his followers had gathered around. They didn't like my answer, and the tension was thick. I told them, "You called me over here and asked me a question. I gave you my answer."

Just then, some of my Christian brothers started to gather around me. I told them, "Go on. I don't need you here. These guys aren't going to do anything."

Nothing happened. They walked away, and so did I.

Respect Through Integrity

Months later, the same leader who had challenged me approached me privately. He told me his wife had suffered a stroke and asked if I would pray for her. It was a humbling moment. Here was a man who didn't share my faith, who had previously challenged me, now seeking prayer from me and my brothers in Christ.

We prayed for his wife, and she recovered. I don't know if it changed his faith, but I do know that moment reflected the respect and trust that God had built through me.

Living by God's Standards

In prison, I refused to live by the protocols or unspoken rules that others followed. If something was wrong, I confronted it. If something needed to be said, I said it. I didn't rely on my strength or cleverness—I relied on God.

Over time, people from all walks of life, even those who didn't like me, came to respect me. They didn't respect me because of my own power but because they saw the boldness and integrity that came from my faith in Christ.

This wasn't about me proving anything to them. It was about living in a way that reflected God's will. When you stand on His word, you don't have to bend to the expectations of others. His will can't be stopped, and His favor will carry you through every challenge.

In Conclusion

The stories in this chapter aren't just about conflicts or victories. They're about how God's will works in practical, everyday life—even in a place as challenging as prison. From standing up for my character to refusing to compromise my beliefs, every moment was an opportunity to trust in God's plan and watch His will unfold.

No matter where you are, God's will is unstoppable. When you align yourself with Him, He gives you the boldness to stand firm, the wisdom to act with integrity, and the favor to overcome challenges that seem insurmountable. And through it all, He uses your life as a testimony to His power and grace.

Chapter 11: Reflection Section: Lessons to Take Away

Here's what I want you to take from this chapter:

- **God's Will is Unstoppable:** When your life is aligned with God's plan, no opposition or circumstance can block what He's set in motion. My experiences in prison are proof that God's purposes prevail, no matter the challenges.
- **Integrity Opens Doors:** Living with integrity, even in tough situations, keeps your character intact it
- invites God's favor. My insistence on that apology wasn't just about me—it was about standing firm in truth and righteousness.
- **Boldness Through Faith:** God gives us the courage to face difficult situations and speak His truth fearlessly. My encounters with other religious groups were moments to demonstrate faith, and through God's strength, I was able to stand firm.
- **Respect is Earned Through Faithful Living:** When you live according to God's standards, your actions will speak louder than words. That's how I gained respect in an environment where it wasn't easily given.

Action Steps for You

Here's how you can apply these lessons in your life:

- **Embrace Integrity:** Decide today to live with integrity in every area of your life, even when it's hard. Trust that God sees and will honor your faithfulness.
- **Stand Firm in Your Faith:** Don't hesitate to stand up for what you believe in. Represent Christ boldly through your words and actions, no matter where you are.
- **Seek God's Will Daily:** Spend time in prayer asking for discernment to understand God's plans for you. Then take steps to follow His direction, even if obstacles arise.

- **Earn Respect Through Love and Service:** Let your actions reflect Christ's love. Serve others selflessly and watch how respect follows a life lived faithfully.

Insights for Prayer

Use these prayer insights to connect with God:

- **Pray for Boldness:** Ask God to help you stand firm in your faith and speak His truth with love, especially when it's uncomfortable.
- **Seek Alignment with God's Will:** Pray for clarity in understanding His plans and the strength to follow them, trusting Him to guide you.
- **Forgiveness and Reconciliation:** If there are broken relationships in your life, bring them to God. Ask Him to help you forgive and to restore what's been damaged.
- **Thank God for His Unstoppable Plan:** Praise Him for His sovereignty and for the assurance that His will is always greater than any challenge you face.

With God's will guiding you and His grace empowering you, there's nothing you can't overcome.

Chapter 11 How Are You Going to Stop God's Will?

Prompt: Reflect on areas where you've tried to control outcomes. Write one or more prayers or steps to surrender control and trust in God's will.

Chapter 12

The Journey Through Rejection

The process of seeking parole is one of the most grueling and disheartening journeys for inmates in Virginia, especially for those incarcerated before 1995. After that year, parole was effectively abolished, requiring inmates to serve at least 85% of their sentence. For those of us still eligible, parole interviews often felt more like a formality than a real chance at freedom. The odds were slim, and many men had been denied parole for decades.

My journey with the parole process began about ten years into my sentence, around 2005. By then, I had already heard countless horror stories from other inmates about how brutal the parole interviews could be. These stories prepared me for what was to come, but they didn't make the process any easier.

Preparing for the First Parole Hearing

Before my first parole hearing, I wanted to understand the process as much as possible. I reached out to my sisters, Dot and Carolyn, asking them to find any resources they could about parole interviews. They sent me books, which I studied carefully. I discovered that Virginia's parole process was modeled after Maryland's system, which aimed to provoke and challenge the inmate.

I learned that the interviewer's goal was to elicit anger or frustration, testing the inmate's temperament. I also knew they wouldn't accept the phrase "I made a mistake" when discussing my crimes. Instead, I had to focus on taking accountability by framing my past actions as bad choices. Armed with this knowledge, I felt prepared for the mental and emotional challenge ahead.

The First Interview

When the day of my first parole hearing came, I was ready. The interviewer—a woman—came in with a demeanor that was cold and confrontational. She drilled me with questions, focusing on the crime that had led to my incarceration. As expected, she wanted detailed explanations and some demonstration of remorse.

I calmly told her about the choices I had made and how I had worked to change since then. I avoided saying I'd made a "mistake" and focused instead on my personal growth and how I was raising my children from prison. When she pressed me about how I could raise my kids from prison, I replied, "Raising a child isn't just about being there to wipe their nose or help with a cold. It's about what you instill in them—values, principles, and guidance."

I shared how I had stayed connected to my children through phone calls and visits. Despite being incarcerated, I was still involved in their lives, to the point where one of their friends told me when I got home he didn't even know I was in prison. He told me my youngest son, would tell him that he needed to talk to me before making a decision about the group they were in. That friend Dominique, said I thought He was coming home and talk to You,

Facing Repeated Rejections

Year after year, I returned to the parole board, and year after year, I faced rejection. The same interviewer came back the next few times, and her approach never changed.

On my second hearing, she wanted to revisit the details of my crime. I refused. "We went over this last year," I told her. "I can't go back and change what I did, but I've done the next best thing—I've changed myself. Let's talk about how I've grown and the steps I've taken to become a better person."

Her persistence didn't waver, but neither did my resolve. By the fifth parole hearing, a different interviewer came in—a man this time. As we talked, he mentioned that he'd read my previous interview notes. "That lady said you were the most introspective person she'd ever interviewed," he told me. Hearing that surprised me, considering how tough she had been, but it didn't change the outcome. I was denied again.

The Fourth Rejection: A Turning Point

When I received my fourth parole denial, I was sitting in my counselor's office. Counselor Ludwig who had delivered all my previous rejections, He handed me the paper and said, "I hate to give you this."

I called my wife to tell her the news. The pain in her voice was unbearable. "They denied you again?" she asked. She barely said anything else. "I can't talk right now," she said before hanging up. Later, I learned how deeply it affected my family. My kids wanted to know what I'd done wrong to deserve another denial. My wife had to explain that it wasn't me—it was the system.

Sitting in my cell after that phone call, I made a decision. I told myself, "There will be no more parole rejections." I wasn't arrogant enough to think I could make this happen on my own. I turned to God, asking Him to guide me through this process and show me what to do to overcome these repeated setbacks.

A New Approach Through Faith

That year, I committed to taking specific steps in my walk with God to prepare for my next parole hearing. I prayed for guidance and clarity, and He answered in ways I hadn't expected.

The first thing He showed me was the power of communion. One morning, as I walked around the yard, another inmate kept looking at his watch. He told me he was heading inside to watch Creflo Dollar on TV. At first I didn't care to go and watch but I felt the Holy Spirit prompting me to watch, too. When I finally gave in

138

and went inside, the message Creflo Dollar was preaching was straight from Zechariah 9:11: "It is the blood of the covenant that sets the prisoners free."

That scripture hit me hard. From that day on, I began taking communion daily. Every morning, I would meditate on the significance of the bread and the wine. I reminded myself that Jesus' body had been broken for me and that His blood sealed a covenant that gave me access to God's power and resources.

Writing My Goals

The next thing God revealed to me was the importance of presenting myself as an individual to the parole board. He instructed me to write down my goals and send them to the board ahead of time. This wasn't just about listing ambitions—it was about showing them who I was and what I intended to do if released.

I prayed over every word I wrote, asking God to let His will guide my plans. My goals were more than just a strategy—they were a testament to the transformation God had worked in me.

The Test of Surrender

Perhaps the most challenging test came when God asked me to pack up all my books and tapes—everything I'd accumulated for my personal growth—and send them home. The instruction was clear: "Send these ahead of you, because you're going home to them."

This was a difficult step of faith. Those materials had been my source of strength and wisdom, and giving them up felt like losing a part of myself. But I obeyed. I boxed up everything and sent it to my family, trusting that God's promise was true.

The Waiting Game

As the date for my next parole hearing approached, I felt a mix of anticipation and peace. I had done everything God had instructed me to do. I had taken communion daily, written my goals, and surrendered my possessions. Now it was in His hands.

This time, I wasn't anxious or fearful. I walked into that hearing with confidence—not in myself, but in the God who had brought me this far.

In Conclusion

The journey through the parole process was a test of faith, perseverance, and trust in God's will. Each rejection brought pain, but it also brought lessons about resilience and dependence on Him.

What I learned through this experience is that God's will is unstoppable. When you align yourself with Him, even the most rigid systems and daunting obstacles can be overcome. It's not about forcing outcomes or relying on your own strength. It's about surrendering to His guidance, obeying His instructions, and trusting that His plans are always greater than ours.

For anyone facing their own "parole process" in life—whether it's a literal prison or a situation that feels just as confining—know this: God's will is not limited by circumstances. When you walk with Him, He will lead you through the trials and into the freedom He has promised.

Chapter 12: Reflection Section: Lessons to Take Away

Let me share some truths from my journey through rejection and faith. I hope these lessons inspire and encourage you:

- **God's Will is Greater Than Man's Systems:** My repeated parole denials taught me that no human system can override God's plans. When we align with His will, even the greatest obstacles will eventually fall in His time.
- **Faith Requires Action:** I didn't just pray for release; I prepared myself by seeking God's guidance, taking communion, and writing down my goals. True faith means trusting God while taking intentional, obedient steps toward His purpose.
- **Rejection Can Be a Tool for Growth:** Each "no" I faced was painful, but it strengthened my trust in God, refined my character, and prepared me for what He had in store. Rejection can be the soil where faith grows.
- **Surrender Brings Breakthrough:** Sending my books and tapes home was an act of surrender and faith. Letting go of something I cherished showed me that trusting God fully often leads to the biggest breakthroughs.

Action Steps for You

Here are some steps you can take as you walk in faith:

- **Respond to Rejection with Faith:** When you face setbacks, don't lose heart. Ask God what He wants you to learn through the experience and trust that He's guiding you toward something greater.
- **Take Practical Steps in Faith:** Partner your prayers with action. Write down your goals, commit them to God, and take consistent steps toward what He's calling you to do.
- **Surrender What You Cling To:** Think about what you're holding onto tightly. Is God asking you to let it go? Trust

Him enough to release it and see what He has in store for you.

- **Focus on Daily Communion:** Make time to take communion regularly, reflecting on Jesus' sacrifice and the promises it secures for you. Let this practice anchor you in faith and hope.

Insights for Prayer

Use these prayer prompts to connect with God during your journey:

- **Pray for Strength During Rejection:** Ask God to help you remain steadfast and faithful when the answers you want seem delayed. Trust in His perfect timing.
- **Seek God's Guidance in Preparation:** Pray for wisdom to align your plans with God's will. Ask Him to show you the steps He wants you to take.
- **Thank God for the Lessons:** Even in painful seasons, thank Him for the growth and preparation He's working in your life. Trust that every challenge is part of His bigger plan.
- **Declare Freedom Through Christ:** Meditate on Zechariah 9:11 and other scriptures that affirm God's ability to set you free. Pray boldly, knowing His promises are for you.

Chapter 12 The Journey Through Rejection

Prompt: Write about areas in your life where you've faced rejection or setbacks. Include one or more goals to turn those experiences into lessons and a prayer for perseverance.

_____
_____
_____
_____
_____
_____
_____
_____
_____
_____
_____
_____
_____
_____
_____
_____
_____
_____
_____
_____
_____

Chapter 13

The Power of Imagination

Proverbs 29:18 says, *"Where there is no vision, the people perish, but happy is he who keeps the law."* This scripture captures one of the most powerful gifts God has given us: the ability to see things before they happen. Whether we use it intentionally or unintentionally, our imagination has the power to shape our reality.

This played out in my life, especially during my last year in prison. The ability to visualize and believe in my freedom wasn't just a tool—it was a weapon. Early in my sentence, I learned to use this gift to combat the temptation of recidivism.

Anthony Robbins says people are motivated by two forces: the desire to avoid pain or the desire to gain pleasure. Most of us are driven by pain, doing whatever we can to escape it. For me, I intentionally associated massive pain with the idea of returning to prison. Even though I had it as good as you could in that environment, the thought of staying there was unbearable.

Turning Pain Into Discipline

I focused on the things I was missing, like my sons' milestones. My oldest son played a basketball game at Southampton High School, just 15 minutes away from the prison. I couldn't be there to see him play. My youngest son started playing football, and I subscribed to the *Virginia Pilot* newspaper just to keep up with his games. Every week, I'd read about how he was doing, knowing he was so close yet completely out of reach.

Both of my sons graduated from schools within an hour of where I was incarcerated, but I couldn't attend either ceremony. The pain of missing those moments was sharp, but it served a purpose. I wasn't punishing myself—I was disciplining myself. I was using that pain to create a barrier against anything that could pull me back into that life.

Years later, when I came home, my youngest son earned his master's degree from the University of North Carolina. I remember how much he wanted me there. The night before graduation

he called and said, "Dad, I don't want any problems. You better be here

Hearing those words made me feel incredible as a father. It showed me how much he valued my presence, and there was no way I was going to let him down. Moments like that reinforced the importance of staying disciplined during my time in prison.

Imagining Freedom

Another tool God showed me was how to use my imagination to bring about change in my life. In the last year of my sentence, I became intentional about visualizing my freedom.

A friend of mine was released on October 24, 2010. Normally another inmate would help someone take their final walk out of the prison by assisting with their belongings. My first thought was not to volunteer. But it's like the Holy Spirit told me to "Take the walk".so I can feel and imagine the exact feelings of waking out the prison.

I changed my mind and I volunteered to help him carry his belongings to the front. As I walked with him, I told myself, *This isn't his walk—this is mine.* I imagined that I was the one being released, feeling the steps, the air, and the moment as if it were my own.

Three months later, on January 28, 2011, I took that walk for real. This time, I went out the gate and never looked back.

That experience taught me the power of visualization. God has given us the ability to see things in our minds before they happen. Unfortunately, most people use this gift to focus on what they don't have or what they fear. But when we use it intentionally to focus on God's promises, it becomes a powerful tool for change.

Imagination as a Weapon

I've used my imagination throughout my life, even in the small things. When I was moved to the honor building at Southampton

147

around my third or fourth year in prison, my room faced a country road. At night, I would watch the cars drive by and imagine myself in one of them, heading home.

More than a decade later, after my release, I drove down that same road and realized I was living the very image I had held onto all those years. I hadn't planned to revisit that road, but when I did, I remembered sitting in my cell, picturing this exact moment.

God showed me that our imagination is one of the most powerful gifts He's given us. It allows us to see and feel the reality of His promises before they come to pass.

Biblical Principles of Imagination

The Bible is full of examples of the power of imagination. In Genesis 11, when the people built the Tower of Babel, God said, *"Nothing they imagine to do will be impossible for them."* This shows how powerful unified vision and imagination can be.

On the other hand, Genesis 6:5 tells us that before the flood, *"The imagination of man's heart was only evil continually."* The people's imagination was so committed to evil that there was no turning back, which led to their destruction.

These scriptures reveal the dual nature of imagination—it can bring forth incredible good or devastating harm, depending on how it's used.

One of my favorite examples of imagination in action comes from Kobe Bryant. Before he ever joined the Lakers, he imagined himself playing for the lakers and having Magic Johnson locker.

148

Years later, he achieved that dream, while becoming one of the greatest players in NBA history.

This principle is true for all of us. Imagination, when combined with faith and action, has the power to change our lives.

Words and Imagination

God created the universe through words, which are essentially the verbal expression of thoughts and images. In Genesis 1, when the earth was formless and void, the Spirit of God hovered over the chaos, imagining what He was about to create. Then He spoke, *"Let there be light,"* and brought order to the chaos.

We are made in God's image, and He has given us the same ability to imagine and speak things into existence. When we align our thoughts and words with His will, we can call forth things that are not as though they were.

Breaking Free Through Imagination

The power of imagination was a critical factor in my release. I began to see myself free, living with my family, and building a new life. I didn't just think about it—I felt it. I experienced the joy of freedom in my mind long before it became a reality.

When the day of my actual release came, it felt almost anticlimactic because I had already lived that moment so many times in my imagination.

If I had known in my first year of prison what I learned in my 16th, the middle years would not have happened But God used those years to teach me and grow my faith. By the time I fully embraced the power of imagination, I was ready to break free—not just physically, but spiritually and mentally.

In Conclusion

Imagination is one of the most powerful tools God has given us. It allows us to see His promises, align our actions with His will, and bring His plans into reality. Whether it's imagining freedom, healing, restoration, or success, this gift can transform our lives when used intentionally.

God showed me how to use imagination to see myself home, united with my family, and living the life He had planned for me. Today, I continue to use this gift, whether it's for personal goals or for impacting others through the books I'm writing with my nephew.

If you're facing challenges, remember this: God has given you the ability to see beyond your circumstances. Use your imagination to focus on His promises, and let Him guide you into the future He has prepared for you.

Chapter 13: Reflection Section: Lessons to Take Away

As we wrap up, let me share some key lessons that can guide you as you move forward in faith:

- **The Power of Vision:** Proverbs 29:18 says, "Where there is no vision, the people perish." This is a powerful reminder of how critical it is to keep God's promises in front of you. Even during my darkest moments, holding on to His vision for my life gave me hope and direction.
- **Imagination is a Gift from God:** God gave us imagination to glimpse His promises before they come to pass. When rooted in faith, it becomes a tool to envision freedom, restoration, or victory, preparing us to receive His blessings.
- **Pain Can Be a Catalyst:** My pain—from missing my sons' milestones to facing rejection—pushed me toward discipline and transformation. God can use pain to propel us into purpose if we allow Him.
- **Faith and Imagination Work Together:** Seeing a better future is important, but pairing that vision with faith and action is what brings it to life. Imagining my freedom kept me focused on God's promises and disciplined in my actions.
- **Words Bring Imagination to Life:** Just as God spoke the world into existence, the words we speak can shape our reality. By declaring God's truth, I aligned my vision with His promises and set the stage for them to unfold.
- **God's Timing is Perfect:** While I wished I had understood these principles earlier, I now see that God's timing was perfect. Every lesson I learned prepared me for lasting freedom and spiritual growth.

Action Steps for You

Here are some practical steps to help you apply these lessons in your own life:

- **Clarify Your Vision:** Take time to pray and reflect on the life God is calling you to. Write down your vision and keep it close as a reminder of His promises.
- **Focus on the Positive:** Shift your thoughts away from fear or negativity. Intentionally focus on God's blessings and His ability to transform your circumstances.
- **Speak Life Over Your Vision:** Declare God's promises over your life. Speak words of life, freedom, and hope, aligning your words with His truth.
- **Turn Pain into Purpose:** Look at areas of pain in your life. Ask God to show you how those struggles can fuel your growth and drive you toward His purpose.

Insights for Prayer

Let these prayer prompts help you seek God's guidance and strength:

- **Pray for Clarity of Vision:** Ask God to open your eyes to His plans for your life and to help you see beyond your current struggles.
- **Meditate on Proverbs 29:18:** Let this verse remind you of the importance of vision and staying aligned with God's Word.
- **Align Your Imagination with God's Word:** Pray for your imagination to be filled with thoughts that reflect His truth and promises, strengthening your faith.

Thank God for His Perfect Timing: Take time to thank Him for the gift of imagination, vision, and the lessons He's teaching you as He prepares you for His promises.

Chapter 13 The Power of Imagination

Prompt: Reflect on how God can use your imagination and vision for His purposes. Write one or more goals for dreaming big and include a prayer asking for His guidance in shaping your dreams.

Chapter 14

God Set Me Free

On April 27, 1995, I stood before a judge who handed me a sentence of 100 years across four charges. Out of those, he suspended 55 years, leaving me with a 45-year active sentence. Even then, it could have been reduced to 20 years if the judge had allowed the sentences to run concurrently. Instead, he made them run consecutively, meaning I had to serve the full 45 years.

To make matters worse, the suspended 55 years hung over my head. If I messed up in any way, that time could be activated and added to my sentence. I walked out of that courtroom defiant—not against the justice system but against the time itself.

In my heart, I told myself, *I will not serve this time. I will not stay here for 45 years.* Even when I learned that Virginia's parole system could release me after 24 or 25 years, I rejected the idea of staying incarcerated for that long.

A Determined Focus

When I first entered prison, I met other inmates who talked about how they had been "set free by God," even while locked up. At first, I didn't fully understand what they meant. But as I began to study God's Word and focus on my own journey, I made a decision: *For the glory of God, I will not serve this sentence in full. I will get out earlier than the state of Virginia says I can.*

This conviction became my focus, my guiding principle. Even though the odds were against me, I believed that God's will and power were greater than the system that held me captive.

The Final Year: A Spiritual Battle

The last year of my incarceration was one of the hardest periods of my life. If you've ever been in an intense spiritual battle, you know the kind of mental and emotional pressure I'm talking about. There were moments when I felt like my mind was caving in under the weight of it all.

Satan used every opportunity to try to convince me that I wasn't going to make it. At my fifth parole hearing, I went up alongside about 30 other inmates. One by one, they received their decisions—every single one of them was turned down.

Satan whispered to me, *Look at all these good men—good Christian men—and they got denied. What makes you think you're any different?*

But I stood my ground. I didn't know why they were turned down, but I refused to believe that my fate would be the same. I told myself, *I will not get a parole turn down. I will not stay in this place.*

I visualized myself at home with my family, free from the walls and fences that surrounded me. I leaned on God's promises and declared His Word over my life.

Understanding Grace

As I fought through that final year, I began to understand grace in a way I never had before. Growing up, I had heard people say, *Grace is unmerited favor,* and that's true. But I came to realize that grace is so much more than that.

Grace, at its core, is a divine influence on the heart. It's not just something we don't deserve—it's something that empowers us. There are two dimensions of grace that I've come to understand.

The first is saving grace. This is the grace that brings us into a relationship with God through Jesus Christ. It's unearned and freely given. When we accept Jesus as our Savior, we move from spiritual separation to union with God.

The second is empowering grace. This is the grace that enables us to overcome challenges, break addictions, and achieve victories in our lives. While saving grace is a gift, empowering grace requires us to act. It demands that we study God's Word, learn His principles, and apply them to our lives.

Activating Grace in My Life

One of the scriptures that became a foundation for me was 2 Peter 1:2, which says, *"Grace and peace be multiplied to you through the knowledge of God and of Jesus our Lord."* This verse showed me that grace isn't just something you receive once—it can grow and multiply in your life as you grow in your knowledge of God.

I realized that if I wanted to experience God's empowering grace, I had to activate it by aligning my actions with His Word. This wasn't something I could do passively—I had to actively participate in my breakthrough.

I remember an older man in prison who used to say, *You've got to challenge your circumstances with the Word of God.* At the time, I didn't fully understand what he meant, but his words stuck with me. Over time, I realized that God's promises weren't just there to read—they were tools to be used in the battles of life.

The Moment of Breakthrough

By the time I reached my fifth parole hearing, my mindset had completely changed. I wasn't afraid of rejection because I knew God was in control.

When I finally received the news that I had made parole, I was overwhelmed with gratitude. The first person I told was a fellow inmate named Ricky White. He had been with me during some of the hardest times, and I wanted him to share in my joy.

After that, I called my wife. When I told her the news, she didn't say much—she just laughed. It was a laugh filled with relief, joy, and gratitude. She had believed with me all along, and now we were finally seeing the fruits of our faith.

Coming Home

My release date was January 28, 2011. My son Lil Randy came to pick me up. He insisted on being the one to pick me up from prison and I will never forget the pride and joy I felt seeing him there. I'll never forget the moment I walked out of those gates. It wasn't just freedom for my body—it was freedom for my mind and spirit.

One of the most emotional moments after my release was reuniting with my family. When I got home, I was amazed by the warm welcome I received. Friends and family came from all over to celebrate my return. One of my friends from high school hugged me so tightly and cried on my shoulder, overwhelmed with emotion. These moments reminded me of the grace and mercy of God, not just in my life but in the lives of those around me.

Even in small moments, like sitting around the table with my family or playing with my grandchildren, I felt an overwhelming sense of gratitude. These were the moments I had imagined during my years in prison, and now they were my reality.

Life After Release

Adjusting to life after prison had its challenges, but God's grace made the transition smoother than I could have imagined. One of the

159

first things I noticed was how fast-paced everything felt. In prison, every day seemed to drag. Life was repetitive and slow, almost like Groundhog Day. But outside, the days flew by.

The advancements in technology were a constant shock. I remember I spent hours figuring out how to use a computer, clicking on everything just to see what would happen. I must have opened a million tabs before my son Randy came over to help clean up the mess I'd made.

Despite these adjustments, I was ready for life outside. I had spent years preparing myself mentally, reading books and learning everything I could. I knew freedom wouldn't be easy, but I also knew I was equipped to handle it.

Adjusting to Freedom

The day I walked out of prison felt almost anticlimactic because, in many ways, I had already experienced that moment in my imagination. Three months before my release, I walked my friend's belongings to the front of the prison as if it were my own exit. That act of visualization made my actual release feel familiar, yet it was still a powerful and emotional moment.

One of the first things I noticed after being released was how fast time seemed to move. In prison, the days felt long because life was repetitive and structured. Every day was like Groundhog Day. But on the outside, everything moved so quickly—it was almost overwhelming at first.

I also had to adjust to changes in technology and society. I remember walking through the mall with my wife and son and seeing people talking to themselves. I said, *What's wrong with these people?* My wife and son laughed and explained that they were using Bluetooth devices. That technology didn't exist when I went to prison, so it was completely foreign to me.

There were other funny moments too. I put my phone on speaker in the middle of the mall, not realizing it wasn't something people typically did. My wife and son thought it was hilarious, but for me, it was just part of adjusting to a new world.

The Value of Freedom

Freedom meant so much more to me after being incarcerated. It wasn't just about being able to go where I wanted or do what I wanted—it was about appreciating the small things.

For example, I could sleep in if I wanted to. I could eat what I wanted when I wanted, rather than being limited to what the prison provided. During my last few years in prison, I had been on a special diet called "common fare," which consisted of vegetables, tuna, and fruits. I chose that diet to avoid the processed foods that many inmates believed were causing health problems. While it was a blessing to have access to healthier options, it was still restrictive compared to the freedom of choosing my meals outside of prison.

When I came home, I had to be careful about how I transitioned back to normal eating. My body had adjusted to raw vegetables and simple meals, so I couldn't immediately jump back into eating everything I wanted. But even with those small challenges, I was grateful for every moment of freedom.

Mental Freedom

One of the biggest lessons I learned during my incarceration was the importance of mental freedom. Early in my sentence, an older man told me, *Put your mind in prison, or you'll never survive.* I told him, *I'll never do that.*

Even though my body was locked up, my mind was never imprisoned. While others saw the barbed wire fences as a symbol of confinement, I looked beyond them and saw freedom. I kept my focus on the future, visualizing myself on the other side of those fences.

This mindset made all the difference. It allowed me to prepare for my release and hit the ground running when I came home.

God's Grace in Action

Looking back, I see how God's grace carried me through every challenge. His grace wasn't just about saving me—it was about empowering me to overcome the obstacles in my path.

When I first entered prison, I couldn't imagine how I would ever make it out. But God showed me that no situation is impossible for Him. He taught me that while there are things we can't do without Him, there are also things He won't do without us. He requires our participation in the breakthroughs we seek.

This partnership with God is something I've carried into every area of my life. Whether it's transitioning back into society, reconnecting with my family, or pursuing new opportunities, I've learned to trust in His guidance and act on His principles.

Lessons Learned

The biggest lesson I learned from my journey is that God is faithful. No matter how impossible a situation may seem, His power is greater than any obstacle.

I also learned the importance of preparation. Freedom isn't just something you step into—it's something you prepare for. During my time in prison, I read books, studied the Bible, and worked on myself so that when the day of my release came, I was ready to embrace it fully.

Finally, I learned the value of community. The love and support of my family, friends, and even strangers reminded me that I wasn't alone in my journey. Their prayers and encouragement helped sustain me during the hardest times.

In Conclusion

My release from prison was more than just a physical event—it was a spiritual and emotional victory. It was a testament to God's grace, the power of faith, and the importance of perseverance.

Today, I live with a renewed sense of purpose. I use my experiences to inspire others, showing them that no matter how dark their circumstances may seem, there is always hope.

God set me free—not just from prison but from the chains of doubt, fear, and hopelessness. And if He can do it for me, He can do it for anyone.

Chapter 14: Reflection Section: Lessons to Take Away

As we close this chapter, here are some key lessons I've learned that I want to share with you:

- **Faith in the Face of Adversity:** No matter how impossible your situation seems, hold fast to God's promises. The moments when the odds feel overwhelming are often when you're closest to your breakthrough.
- **God's Grace is Empowering:** Grace is more than unmerited favor—it's the divine power to overcome. Stay rooted in His Word, and let His principles guide your steps.
- **Declare and Visualize Victory:** I often envisioned myself free and reunited with my family. By aligning your thoughts and words with God's truth, you prepare your heart to receive what He has promised.
- **Your Freedom is in Your Mind:** Even when I was physically confined, I didn't allow my mind to be imprisoned. Where the Spirit of the Lord is, there is freedom, and that freedom starts within you.
- **Perseverance in Prayer and Action:** God calls us to participate in His plans. Through consistent prayer, study, and obedience, you can activate His promises and see them come to pass.
- **Surround Yourself with Encouragement:** My journey wouldn't have been the same without my wife, family, and mentors. Surround yourself with people who will strengthen your faith and help you stay on course.

Action Steps for You

Let me challenge you to take these steps this week:

- **Reflect on God's Promises:** What's one challenge you're facing right now? Find a promise in God's Word that speaks to it and hold on to that truth.

- **Apply Grace:** Think of an area where you need to extend grace, whether to yourself or someone else. Pray for God to strengthen you in this.
- **Visualize Your Breakthrough:** Picture your victory as already achieved. In your prayer time, thank God as though it's already done and trust in His perfect timing.

Insights for Prayer

Here are some prayer prompts to help you connect with God as you reflect on these lessons:

- **Pray for Faith in Adversity:** Ask God to give you clarity and strength to trust Him, even in your darkest moments.
- **Meditate on 2 Corinthians 3:17:** "Where the Spirit of the Lord is, there is freedom." Let this verse remind you to release mental and emotional burdens to Him.
- **Activate God's Grace:** Pray for His empowering grace to flow in your life as you apply biblical principles and move toward transformation.
- **Seek Guidance and Encouragement:** Ask God to surround you with wise counsel and to guide your actions as you persevere in faith and prayer.

Know this: God's promises for your life are good, and His grace is sufficient to carry you through every trial. Stay faithful, and watch Him work.

Chapter 14 Prompt: God Set Me Free

Prompt: Reflect on areas where you seek freedom—spiritually, emotionally, or physically. Write one or more goals for achieving this freedom and include a prayer for God's guidance.

Chapter 15

Grace Beyond Bars

The Journey of Parole and Favor

When I came home, I faced both parole and probation. Each was meant to last twenty years. But by God's favor, I was released from one within three years and the other shortly after. Instead of decades, I walked free from those restrictions in just five years.

The favor I experienced on parole was unusual. Many men face heavy restrictions—curfews, limited travel, constant check-ins—but my experience was different. Right from the start, my parole officer gave me an unusual level of trust. Less than a month after being released, I traveled to New York, Pennsylvania, and Dallas.

Most parolees were restricted to a 35-mile radius, yet I was allowed to go anywhere within Virginia. My parole officer told me, *If you need to cross state lines, just let me know, and I'll get you a travel permit to be safe.* That kind of freedom wasn't normal, but it showed the level of favor I was walking in.

A friend of mine, who also made parole, had to wait for approval just to buy a car out of state. Meanwhile, I was traveling freely without any issues. This was nothing short of the grace of God.

Divine Connections and Early Release

God was working for me the first time my parole officer came to visit my house. As soon as he walked in, he noticed a picture of my niece on the wall. He said, *I went to school with her. Is that your niece?*

Yes, that's my niece, I replied.

That connection shifted everything. He was already a good man, but from that moment, our relationship grew even stronger. He went above and beyond for me, helping me get off parole early. Before leaving his position for private business, he ensured I had the freedom I needed.

This wasn't just about luck; it was God's plan. Another friend of mine had talked to this parole officer before my release, asking him to take my case. God was working behind the scenes, orchestrating favor in ways I couldn't have imagined.

Returning to the Church

Shortly after coming home, I visited Gospel Temple, a church I had known before my incarceration. While I was there, the pastor called me into his office. He congratulated me on being home, then said something that took me by surprise.

"Randy, I know what kind of person you were before. But I also know God, and I can see the change in You, He offered me the privilege to minister at The New Gospel Temple

I was stunned. Here was someone who had known me in my wildest days, opening the doors of ministry to me without hesitation.

God had told me during my incarceration that He would raise me up to teach and guide others. He said, *The sister'at the church didn't help you because she didn't know how. But I'm going to send you back to teach there.* That moment with the pastor confirmed what God had spoken to me years earlier.

Restoration in My Family

One of the greatest miracles I experienced after coming home was the restoration of my relationship with Annette. Before I went to prison, our marriage had its struggles. During a visiting room conversation, I told her, *You need to learn how to love a man.*

Her response was simple but honest: *I do, because I've never had a man before.*

We'd been married for over twenty years at that point, but her words made me realize how much we both had to learn. It wasn't until I truly grew in Christ that I became the husband she needed.

By God's grace, our relationship began to heal even before my release. But being home allowed us to grow even closer. We started to understand each other in ways we never had before, and our love deepened through the process.

Reunited with the Community

Coming back to my community was overwhelming in the best way. Almost everyone welcomed me with open arms, as if I had never been gone.

One of the most emotional moments came when I ran into my high school basketball coach. He saw me in a store with my wife, froze, and sat down. He stared at me for what felt like forever before saying, *I'm so glad to see you. I've got my son back.*

I hugged him and said, *Coach, do you remember how much I hated losing? Do you remember how hard I fought to win a basketball game?*

He nodded, and I continued, *If I fought that hard for a game, how much harder do you think I fought to win my life back?*

He smiled and said again, *I've got my son back.*

Those moments reminded me of how much people cared and how far God had brought me.

The Weight of Loss

Coming home was a blessing, but it was also marked by loss. Many family members who had been a part of my life before my incarceration were no longer here. The absence of my mother hit the hardest.

When my mom passed away, I struggled with God. I couldn't understand why He hadn't shown me she was sick. I prayed and asked, *Lord, You've shown me so many things while I've been in here. Why didn't You show me this?*

The Holy Spirit gently reminded me, *If you had known, you would have prayed for her to stay. But she's better off with Me.*

That revelation brought me peace, even though it didn't take away the pain. I realized that my prayers would have been selfish trying to keep her here when she was ready to go home to the Lord.

God's Grace in Action

God's grace wasn't just evident in my release; it was evident in the opportunities He gave me afterward. I've had the privilege of speaking in churches, sharing my testimony, and encouraging others. One of the most meaningful experiences was returning to Middle Spring, the church I grew up in.

I've spoken there multiple times, each time feeling the weight of what it meant to stand in that pulpit. My parents loved that church, and it was a blessing to honor their memory by sharing God's word with the congregation.

Freedom Redefined

For me, freedom means more than just being out of prison. It's about living a life that honors God and takes full advantage of the opportunities He provides. It's about cherishing the simple things—

like sleeping in if I want to, eating what I want when I want, and spending time with my family.

Freedom also means recognizing the value of every moment. I never take for granted the ability to drive down the road, visit my family, or simply sit outside and enjoy the day.

The Ultimate Lesson

The biggest lesson I've learned is that there's no situation too hard for God. His grace is sufficient, and His power is limitless. But I also learned that we have to cooperate with Him. There are things He won't do without us.

During my incarceration, I refused to let my mind be imprisoned. My body may have been behind bars, but my spirit was free. I focused on the other side of the barbed wire, on the freedom I knew I would one day walk in.

Now that I'm home, I see the fruits of that mindset. My family is restored, my community has welcomed me back, and I have the privilege of sharing my story to inspire others.

In Closing

Grace isn't just about getting what we don't deserve—it's about being empowered to live a life that reflects God's goodness. My journey from incarceration to freedom is a testament to that truth.

No matter how far you've fallen or how impossible your situation seems, God's grace is available to you. He can turn your pain into purpose, your mistakes into miracles, and your struggles into testimonies.

I'm living proof of what God can do when you trust Him.

Chapter 15: Reflection Section: Lessons to Take Away

Here's what I want you to take from this chapter:

- **God's Favor Breaks Barriers:** My experience of receiving early parole and the unexpected freedoms I encountered remind us that God's favor can overcome even the most rigid systems. When God opens a door, no one can close it.
- **Divine Connections Matter:** From a parole officer with a connection to my family to friends advocating for me, I've seen how God uses relationships to accomplish His plans. Trust Him to bring the right people into your life.
- **Restoration is Possible:** No matter how broken a relationship may seem, God can restore it. He did it in my marriage with Annette and with my children, and He can do it for you, too.
- **Live Free in Your Spirit:** True freedom starts in your heart and mind. Even when I was behind bars, I focused on the freedom God promised me, which prepared me to live fully when I was released.
- **God's Grace is Transformative:** His grace didn't just forgive me—it empowered me to rebuild my life and help others. It's through His grace that we're able to step into the lives He's called us to.
- **The Importance of Preparation:** I spent years preparing mentally, spiritually, and practically for the life I wanted after prison. When freedom came, I was ready to embrace it and walk in my purpose.

Action Steps for You

Here are some steps to help you apply these lessons:

- **Reflect on Restrictions:** Think about areas where you feel stuck or held back. Pray and ask God to reveal His favor and guide you toward freedom, whether it's emotional, spiritual, or physical.

- **Pursue Restoration:** Identify a relationship that needs healing. This week, take one step—whether it's offering an apology, initiating a conversation, or praying for the other person.
- **Embrace God's Grace:** Picture your life fully aligned with God's grace. Speak His promises over your circumstances, believing in His power to transform your life.

Insights for Prayer

- **Pray for Awareness of Favor:** Ask God to help you recognize His favor in your life and trust Him to work through even the smallest details.
- **Meditate on 2 Corinthians 12:9:** "My grace is sufficient for you, for my power is made perfect in weakness." Let this verse remind you of God's strength working in and through you.
- **Pray for Restoration:** Bring broken relationships to God in prayer and trust Him to bring healing, no matter how impossible it seems.
- **Thank God for Freedom in Christ:** Reflect on the freedom Jesus provides and commit to living in a way that honors Him in your daily life and long-term choices.

God's grace has carried me through challenges, opened doors I couldn't imagine, and transformed my life. I pray it does the same for you.

Chapter 15 Grace Beyond Bars

Prompt: Reflect on the overarching message of God's grace in your life. Write one or more ways to live out this grace daily and include a prayer of gratitude and commitment.

Epilogue

I want to thank You for reading this book. I hope it has the effect on You that I envisioned when I wrote it.

This book was not meant to be a biography of my troubles in life, but a narrative of how we can partner with God no matter our circumstances and truly be what He has made us to be — overcomers! God is not a respecter of persons. The favor and grace that He showed me is also available for You, the reader.

However, it does require Your participation with God. I can assure You from experience that no matter what You may be facing, with God, you can defeat it.

My heartfelt desire for You is that You will partner with God all the time and experience the life He has for You.

With sincere gratitude,

Randy

Receive His Grace

A Heartfelt Invitation to Grace

As I sit here reflecting on the journey God has taken me on, I want to extend to you the greatest gift I've ever received: the grace of God. It doesn't matter where you are right now—whether you're in a cell, in a tough season, or simply searching for something more—God's grace is big enough, strong enough, and real enough to meet you right where you are.

Grace isn't something you earn or work for. It's a gift—a free, undeserved gift of love, forgiveness, and redemption. And the beauty of it is that God's grace doesn't care about your past. It doesn't care about your failures, your mistakes, or even how far you feel from Him. It only cares about one thing: your heart.

Jesus Christ came into this world to give you hope, to set you free, and to offer you a new life. He gave His life so that you could have yours, not weighed down by guilt or regret, but filled with purpose, peace, and joy.

If you feel that tug in your spirit, that whisper telling you that now is the time to surrender, don't ignore it. That's God calling you into His arms. All you have to do is say yes.

Here's a simple prayer to start:

"Lord Jesus, I come to You just as I am. I ask You to forgive me of my sins and come into my life. I believe You died for me,

and I believe You rose again. I surrender my heart to You and ask You to guide me, transform me, and teach me how to live in Your grace. Thank You for loving me. Thank You for saving me. In Jesus' name, Amen."

If you prayed that prayer, know this—you are now part of God's family. You are forgiven. You are free. And the grace that saved you will now carry you through every trial and every challenge you face.

Welcome to a new beginning. God loves you, and so do I.

With all my heart,

Randy White

Your Vision Journal

This section is designed to help you capture your dreams, goals, and reflections as you align your life with God's vision for you. Use the prompts below to guide your entries and ignite your imagination:

1. Write down a specific promise from God that you're holding onto.
2. What is one relationship you hope to see restored?
3. Describe the person you feel God is calling you to become.
4. What areas of your life need God's transformation?
5. What dream has God placed on your heart that seems impossible?
6. Reflect on a time when God showed you His favor—what happened?
7. What are three goals you want to achieve in the next year?
8. What habits or mindsets are holding you back from God's best?
9. What is one way you've seen God's grace in your life this week?
10. Write about a scripture that inspires your faith journey.
11. Who has God placed in your life to guide or encourage you?
12. What are you most grateful for today?
13. What steps can you take this week to grow closer to God?
14. What does "freedom in Christ" look like for you?
15. Where do you see God leading you in the next five years?
16. What pain in your life could God be using for a greater purpose?
17. What legacy do you want to leave for your family and community?
18. How can you serve others and reflect God's love this week?
19. What is one fear you need to release to God?
20. What victory has God already given you that you can celebrate today?

Take time to write, reflect, and pray over your entries. Let this journal become a space where you document God's work in your life, envision His plans for your future, and deepen your faith in His promises.

Write your dreams, goals, or reflections here
(e.g. - What is one relationship you hope to see restored? Why?)

_____

_____
_____
_____
_____
_____
_____
_____
_____
_____
_____
_____
_____
_____
_____
_____
_____
_____
_____
_____
_____
_____
_____
_____
_____

Write your dreams, goals, or reflections here

Write your dreams, goals, or reflections here

Write your dreams, goals, or reflections here

Write your dreams, goals, or reflections here

Write your dreams, goals, or reflections here

Write your dreams, goals, or reflections here

Write your dreams, goals, or reflections here

Write your dreams, goals, or reflections here

Author Bio

Randall White, author of 'Grace Beyond Bars,' transformed his life after overcoming a 100-year prison sentence through the supernatural grace of God. He excelled in prison ministry, where he established new ministries and taught the Word of God. Randall continues to speak in prisons today. A devoted husband to Annette White and father of two, Randall believes wholeheartedly in the transformative power of God's Word. His mission is to empower those who feel hopeless and share his testimony of redemption through the true and living God. Randall is a mentor to many, focusing on being a teacher in the Kingdom of God and spreading the message of God's grace.

About Build Our Kingdom Publishing

Build Our Kingdom Publishing, established in 2020, is dedicated to producing impactful Christian and business publications. Our mission is to bring more people to Christ and build them up in the Kingdom of God. Visit buildourkingdom.com to learn more about our authors and our mission.

Books Available Soon
Grace to Succeed

"Grace to Succeed" explores the profound principles of biblical success, teaching readers how to experience true achievement

through God's grace. This book goes beyond monetary gain, emphasizing the divine connection needed to fulfill one's purpose. Randy dives deep into scripture to guide readers in aligning their lives with God's plan, demonstrating that success isn't just about what you achieve but how you walk in His grace. Through practical insights and spiritual wisdom, this book shows that lasting success comes when you know God and live out His purpose.

Grace Beyond Failure

"Grace Beyond Failure" is a transformative book for anyone who feels weighed down by past mistakes, overwhelming regret, or  the fear of failing again. This inspiring guide reveals how God's grace meets you in the midst of your greatest challenges and empowers you to turn failure into a stepping stone for growth.

Rather than letting failure define you, *Grace Beyond Failure* encourages you to embrace it as an opportunity to uncover new strength, deepen your faith, and pursue a better future. Through practical wisdom, biblical insights, and personal reflection, the book equips you to rise above the shame of failure and discover the grace that carries you toward victory.

Whether you've made mistakes that seem impossible to recover from or you're scared to take risks because of past missteps, this book will show you how to lean on God's grace to overcome every obstacle. With *Grace Beyond Failure,* you'll learn to run your race with purpose, resilience, and faith.

Grace in Prison

Grace in Prison is a powerful and uplifting guide designed specifically for inmates, offering a pathway to transformation

through the boundless grace of God. Written by someone who has experienced life behind bars and discovered God's unrelenting love, this book provides a message of hope, renewal, and purpose for those navigating their prison journey.

Through practical teaching and heartfelt encouragement, *Grace in Prison* shows inmates how to embrace God's grace in every aspect of their lives—how to receive it, live it, and walk in it daily. From learning to forgive themselves and others to finding strength in God's promises, this book equips readers with the spiritual tools to grow closer to God, even in the most challenging circumstances.

More than just a guide, this book is a call to transformation, reminding inmates that their time in prison can be a season of growth, healing, and preparation for the future. *Grace in Prison* will inspire you to overcome, to live fully in God's grace, and to emerge with a renewed sense of purpose and identity in Christ.

Grace Over Addiction

Grace Over Addiction is a transformative guide written by someone who has walked the painful road of addiction and emerged

on the other side through the power of God's grace. This book is more than just a testimony—it's a roadmap for anyone seeking hope and healing in the midst of their struggles. With raw honesty and spiritual insight, the author shares how God's unrelenting love can reach into even the darkest corners of life and provide a path to freedom.

You'll discover practical steps grounded in biblical principles, stories of redemption, and the tools needed to rebuild your life on a foundation of faith. *Grace Over Addiction* reminds readers that no matter how far you've fallen, God's grace is deeper still. Whether you're seeking recovery for yourself or supporting someone on their journey, this book offers encouragement, hope, and the assurance that through God, true transformation is possible.

8 Ways to Avoid Mental Trappings of the World

Eight Ways to Avoid Mental Trappings of the World by Randall White is a transformative guide to breaking free from the mental

snares set by Satan and the devices he uses to keep people spiritually bound. Drawing from deep biblical truths and practical insights, this book equips readers with the tools they need to recognize and overcome the enemy's tactics in their daily lives.

Randall White unveils eight powerful strategies to help you guard your mind, discern lies from truth, and stay rooted in God's Word amidst the distractions and deceptions of the world. From confronting fear and doubt to breaking cycles of negativity, each chapter provides actionable steps to fortify your mind against spiritual attacks.

This book is a call to freedom, empowering you to reclaim your thoughts, align them with God's truth, and live with renewed clarity and purpose. *Eight Ways to Avoid Mental Trappings of the World* will inspire you to walk boldly in God's wisdom and resist the schemes of the enemy.

Want to get in contact with Randy

Email

RandallW861@gmail.com

www.ingramcontent.com/pod-product-compliance
Lightning Source LLC
Chambersburg PA
CBHW071729120626
46550CB00002B/444